Queen Of Hearts

A story of mothers and daughters,
what we inherit, and what we pass on

By Florence St John

La Maison Publishing, Inc.
Vero Beach, Florida
The Hibiscus City

Maison

"You are the bows from which your children, as living arrows, are sent forth."
                                    Kahlil Gibran

Monsters Under the Bed

The low moans from my daughter's room woke me in the middle of the night. Her muffled cries filtered through the wall, growing louder in the darkness. I turned to my husband, Edward, but his side of the bed was empty. He was never around when a crisis hit. I didn't trust his parenting methods anyway. He had a way of making people feel inadequate. Alone, I tiptoed into the hall and opened the door. The digital clock cast a faint red glow.

"Are you all right, Annmarie?" I smoothed her quilt, bunched at her feet, then sat on the edge of her bed. "What's wrong?"

"I hate high school," she sobbed. "I hate the kids, the teachers, and my life!"

"Why? What happened?"

"Everyone makes fun of me, especially the boys. They say I'm skinny and I have a big nose."

"Have you told the teachers?"

"They don't care. The teachers love the popular kids, and I'm not one of them."

"In two years, you'll never see these kids again," I said as the heat kicked on with a whoosh. "Can't you just focus on your schoolwork until you graduate?"

"I'm not going to graduate! I'm failing."

"Failing? You've always earned straight As."

"That was when I was in middle school. The work is harder now, especially in math."

"Math was my worst subject, too," I said. "When I was struggling, my father hired a math teacher who came to the house every week. We can hire a tutor."

"It won't help! I can't do it!"

"Don't give up. We can try."

"Face it," she snapped. "I'm just stupid!"

"You're not stupid," I said. "Get some rest. We'll figure it out in the morning. I promise."

Usually, I was good at problem-solving, but I couldn't fix this particular issue. Teenagers could be cruel, and teachers sometimes didn't realize the damage their verbal attacks could cause to a young mind. After thinking about it all night and getting very little sleep, I decided the best solution was to pull Annmarie out of school for the rest of the year. She would be held back a grade, but at least she would have time to catch up with her class.

She loved the idea, so I scheduled a parent-teacher conference.

Annmarie and I felt hopeful as we drove to the school for the meeting. The teachers were already in the conference room. Mrs. McKean, the math teacher; Mr. Russell, who taught science and physical education; Miss Clark, the English teacher; and Mr. Marlin, who taught history and social studies, sat around the table with their coffee mugs half-empty, indicating they had started the discussion before we arrived. They became quiet as we entered. Overhead, fluorescent lights flickered, casting the room in a harsh white glow.

Annmarie sat in the empty chair at the head of the table. I took a seat to her right.

Mrs. McKean spoke first. "We're a little confused, Mrs. St. John. Why did you request this meeting?"

"Annmarie's been a little depressed lately. She's having trouble keeping up with her schoolwork. She's fallen behind and is afraid she may fail. I'd like to withdraw her from school."

"If she withdraws midyear, she'll lose credits, which will trigger a truancy process," Miss Clark protested.

"I'm not talking about dropping out of school. It would be only until the end of sophomore year, giving Annmarie time to catch up on her studies. She can start fresh next year."

"She's a smart girl," Mr. Marlin said. "I hate to see her held back a grade."

Sweat pooled at the base of my neck. "She's only sixteen. What difference does it make if she graduates a year later?"

Mr. Russell scratched his head. "It seems you want to take the easy way out, but that's a bad idea."

As her mother, I could push it—but I began to doubt myself. *What if they were right?*

"Annmarie doesn't need to quit school," Mrs. McKean insisted. "She just needs to apply herself."

"Now that we know there's a problem, we can help her," Miss Clark offered. "What do you say, Annmarie? Will you let us help you?"

Annmarie nodded, staring at the floor. Her agreement settled it. She would remain in school, and her teachers would give her extra time afterward. They escorted her to her second-period class, but the look on my daughter's face was one of submission. I left the school feeling more confused than resolved. It wasn't supposed to turn out this way. I had always been Annmarie's hero, and she depended on me to save her.

~2~

Over the next couple of months, I assumed Annmarie was doing better in school because there were no more complaints about the other kids. She spent most of her time in her room and no longer confided in me. I sensed her slipping away.

"How's everything going?" I asked one day.

"Fine, Mother!" she snapped.

I could smell cigarette smoke wafting off her when she came home from school. I wasn't sure whether to confront her, but I couldn't ignore my concern.

"Your clothes smell of cigarettes," I said. "Have you been smoking, Annmarie?"

"No," she said, though I had my doubts. "It would be awful if you fell into that dirty habit. Besides, you're the one who convinced me to stop smoking five years ago."

"You never trust me!" she said, then dashed up the stairs to her room.

"I'm sorry. It's just …" I had crossed a line. I wanted to believe Annmarie. She thought I didn't trust her, but I felt she didn't trust me.

A gnawing urgency compelled me to enter her sacred domain—her room—the next day, when she was at school. It was a disaster; clean and dirty clothes were piled in the corner, and old, crusty plates of food sat on the nightstand. Ashtrays, filled with cigarette butts, were hidden under her bed. I sighed as I collected the dirty dinnerware. Then I saw something dark against the carpet—a thin, rust-colored trail. It led to a towel crumpled on the floor. When I picked it up, the stiff fabric crackled in my hands.

Horrified, I called my son, who was home from school with a cold. Joseph came into the room and stared at the towel. He showed no surprise.

"Do you know what this is?" I asked.

"She cuts herself," he said, as if he were telling me she had forgotten her homework.

"Cuts? You mean with a knife?"

"Mostly razors," my son replied casually. "But I saw her do it with a key once. She's been cutting herself for months."

My stomach dropped—not because I didn't believe him, but because I did.

"Why?"

"Because she's crazy!"

"No, she isn't!" I said, more for me than for him.

Lately, she was so angry it scared me, but hurting herself? I convinced myself it was an isolated incident, but recalled when she was five. Whenever she felt overwhelmed, she bit her arm. The crescent of teeth marks bloomed on her arm.

A children's book — It's Okay to Be Angry — sat on her shelf, its pages dog-eared from repeated reading.

I wasn't ready to face the truth, but reality wouldn't let me hide for long. A call from the school left me seated in the main office.

"Thank you for coming, Mrs. St. John," the counselor said. "We're concerned about your daughter. Other girls noticed cuts on her arms. One girl witnessed her slicing her skin with a sharp object."

I winced. Something was so wrong that my baby felt compelled to hurt herself.

"Do you think she's capable of suicide?" the school counselor asked.

"No, I don't think so," I said, but I wasn't sure anymore.

It felt like the monster had been under our bed the whole time — and I'd been stepping around it in the dark.

"I think you should take her to see a psychologist." She gave me the name and number of a therapist. I promised to call, but I was reluctant. My mother had always been adamant that no one in our family air our dirty laundry to strangers, fearing that any label would carry consequences.

Annmarie seemed to get worse as the weeks went by. She lashed out in anger every day, and our fights grew more volatile and frequent. The fear that she would continue cutting herself hung over my head. I couldn't bear the thought of more scars, so I backed down.

Determined to solve this on my own, I took on her depression as if it were the fight of my life. I was stunned to learn how many other girls were suffering from the same problem. I scoured the internet for everything I could find on "cutting." Online, everything had a name. The term BPD—borderline personality disorder—kept appearing. I didn't know enough to diagnose my daughter, but it seemed to fit her personality and behavior. The words blazed across my screen, searing into my mind. Was this a real medical diagnosis or just psychobabble? Was it inherited? Passed on? Curable? All I knew was that it carried a heavy stigma and promised a future of dysfunction.

The more I read, the more things in my life began to make sense. Memories flashed through my mind, revealing patterns and phases that mirrored what I saw online. I began comparing the personality traits of my mother, my sisters, my daughter, and me. There were similarities, but not every behavior pointed to a disorder. The women in my family showed borderline tendencies, but beneath that lay low self-esteem and codependency.

Codependency! I had always rolled my eyes at the term.

So what exactly is codependency? I found a series of codependency tests. Out of curiosity, I took one. It had ten simple yes-or-no questions, and I answered yes to all of them.

1. Home was not safe. You grew up in a dysfunctional home. Your parents were addicts and/or constantly fighting.

2. Who Cares? You were invisible at home. What you said didn't matter.

3. Their Unhappiness Became Mine. Love meant accommodating someone else's needs.

4. Other People Come First. You minimize your own needs and overextend yourself to earn approval.

5. Mature child. You grew up quickly to take care of your siblings or to stay off your parents' radar while they were fighting.

6. Saying 'No' means you don't love me. You think it's selfish to say 'No,' and you end up in situations you later resent.

7. Nothing you do is ever good enough. You have low self-esteem. You jumped through hoops to please your parents.

8. Conflict Avoidance.
You tend to apologize or take the blame to keep the peace. Overwhelming fears of rejection and/or abandonment.

9. Controlling Love. Your parents' affection was given and withdrawn based on your usefulness.

10. You Didn't Fit In
You didn't feel comfortable in your own skin and couldn't relate to other kids.

I stared at the computer screen long after the words stopped making sense. Codependency. Dysfunctional family. Borderline traits. The language felt clinical, almost cold, yet each sentence described my life with unsettling accuracy. I had opened the search hoping to understand my daughter, but the spotlight had somehow shifted to me.

Annmarie's bloodstained towel lay folded in my mind like evidence I couldn't ignore. I kept asking the same question: What had I missed? I had loved her fiercely, protected her, and tried to fix every problem before it could hurt her. Yet somehow she was in pain so deep it carved into her skin.

The thought settled heavily in my chest. *What if this didn't start with her? What if it started with me?*

Part One
At the Core

Until that moment, I had believed parenting was a shield — that if you loved your child enough, you could spare them the wounds you carried. Now I wondered whether children inherit more than eye color and mannerisms.

I remembered the counselor's voice suggesting therapy and my immediate resistance. In my family, we survived by not talking. We buried things, minimized them, laughed them off, or prayed them into submission. Looking back was dangerous. It threatened loyalties and exposed truths no one wanted named.

But Annmarie was slipping away from me. If I wanted to understand why my daughter felt broken, I needed to understand the world that shaped the mother she had grown up with. I had to examine the lessons I had learned long before I ever held her in my arms — the ones I unknowingly carried into my own parenting.

Memories I had carefully packed away began to surface. Scenes I hadn't revisited in decades returned with startling clarity. The smell of Scotch in the air, whispered arguments behind closed doors, and the constant feeling of walking on eggshells. Moments I once dismissed as "normal" suddenly looked different in the harsh light of recognition.

Before I could understand my daughter's wounds, I needed to remember my own.

So I went back.

Before I became Annmarie's mother, I was a girl named Florence. Even then, I was learning how to survive in a world full of chaos. The memories didn't come back gently. They returned in flashes — sounds and fears.

One of my earliest memories is of a family wedding when I was four. My cousin Lea and I wore matching ruffled dresses and shiny white patent-leather shoes. Our socks had white lace trim at the cuffs. We were the center of attention as we twirled, making our dresses swish and swirl. I felt special, like I mattered just as much as she did.

My mother looked radiant, gliding across the dance floor with her cousins.

Meanwhile, my father sat at our table, drinking Scotch on the rocks until a jealous rage overtook him and he cut the evening short.

Driving home intoxicated, he stomped on the gas and accused my mother of flirting. The car swayed as he sped around the curves. "Please, Daddy, don't," I whispered, crouched on the backseat floor, praying we wouldn't die.

My father had many sides. Sometimes he was loving and warm, everything I wanted a father to be. He lifted me onto his shoulders or tickled me until my stomach hurt.

Beneath his alcoholism, a spark of creativity sometimes ignited into a flame. He could draw, paint, invent, write poetry — and build the wildest projects.

While we all slept at night, he sat in the living room, smoking cigarettes and drawing cartoon characters. I would wake up to find the drawings on the coffee table.

I couldn't believe my father had produced these wonders, and I welled up with pride.

The tension stayed close to the surface.

He called my mother a "pinhead" when he was trying to be funny and a "c**t" when he was drunk. I didn't know what the word meant, only that it hurt.

The anger behind it twisted in my stomach. We barricaded ourselves in a bedroom while he pounded on the door.

When I thought I couldn't hate him more, he began to cry. I didn't want to see him sad. Somehow, that was worse.

My mother often sighed and said, "After all I sacrificed—"

The Brooklyn winters felt as unpredictable as my father's moods. Ice lingered on the streets, and fresh snow packed over what never fully melted. I remember sitting in the living room with my brother. We stayed bundled in coats indoors, waiting for the heat to come back on, careful not to complain. The furnace kept breaking down, and my mother boiled water on the stove so we could wash our clothes.

One Christmas morning, Santa brought my brother a sled. After our mother bundled us in snowsuits, boots, and mittens, my father took us outside to show us how it worked.

"Watch how I do it," he said.

We stood on the curb as he took a running start, hopped on the sled, and zoomed down the ice-covered road. He was flying!

We were impressed. Look at Dad go! I thought.

The sled jerked suddenly; it was no longer beneath him. It had snagged on a piece of cardboard beneath the ice. He maintained his reckless pace down the hill until he reached the bottom, a bloody mess. His chin had split open on the ice, requiring six stitches. We stood frozen on the curb, unsure whether to run toward him or away.

Neither my brother nor I got to ride. We never saw that sled again. It was better not to expect too much.

~3~

My parents slept on a pull-out bed in the living room. Some nights, they laughed, and I fell asleep easily. Other nights, my brother and I clung to each other, waiting for the shouting to end.

We moved often from one apartment to another, and my father cleaned buildings in exchange for free rent. I remember one on 45th Street in Brooklyn, where the lobby walls were covered with floor-to-ceiling mirrors on all sides. I'd stand in the middle and watch my reflection. Sometimes I wondered which reflection was the real me.

My sister's baby carriage was stored under the stairs. Her crib was placed in the corner of the room, close enough so I could hear her breathing at night. It felt like my world was closing in.

At night, it followed me into my dreams. The witch from *Snow White* appeared, holding out the apple. I couldn't refuse it.

Sometimes I woke up to the smell of cooking food and saw them laughing quietly in the kitchen. I stayed in the doorway until they noticed me and waved me in. Sometimes, I was allowed to stay awake later than my siblings, and I cherished those stolen moments with my mother before she sent me to bed.

In a crowded family, closeness came in scraps. So when she took me to the movies, just the two of us, it felt less like an outing and more like a gift.

I followed her down the dimly lit aisle, clutching the box of candy she had bought at the concession stand. We slipped into our seats in the front row. The screen looked enormous. The lights dimmed, and the theater grew quiet, except for the rustle of popcorn and whispered voices.

The movie was *Whatever Happened to Baby Jane!*

Faces loomed large on the screen. I shrank into my seat, frightened by the flickering images. Every so often, I looked sideways at my mother. Her face was illuminated by the screen's glow.

Even though I was scared, I didn't want to leave. Time alone with her was rare, and I wished it could last as long as possible.

When the movie ended, and the lights came up, I felt both relieved and sad. The film was over. Soon we would go home, and she'd belong to everyone again.

But during those two hours, she was completely mine.

We moved into a brownstone on 71st Street. Dad built an apartment in the basement for my grandfather, complete with its own bathroom and kitchen. I felt bad for him because he looked sad. Only a wall separated him from the roar of the furnace on the other side of the basement. When it kicked on with a bang, my brother and I thought it was a monster and ran upstairs. After a while, we got used to the sound.

Our house was next to a telephone company. In the yard, there was a fence that separated our home from the alley. Sometimes, I slipped through a hole in the wire fence to play there. I felt safer alone.

In first grade, I walked to school alone before I understood why no one walked with me. I climbed the stairs to the El, crossed through the station, and came down the other side toward PS 112. In winter, we stood in the courtyard, jumping up and down to stay warm while we waited for the bell.

When it rang, we marched inside in pairs. The building was old, with cinder-block walls in the hallways and small wooden desks in the classrooms. The other children were loud, running around the room and talking over each other. I sat frozen at my desk.

Every morning, we stood by our desks and recited the Pledge of Allegiance. I moved my lips, but no sound came out. I didn't seem to have a voice, or maybe I was afraid to speak it.

School had rules, and I quickly learned how to follow them. If we needed to go to the bathroom, we raised our hands and waited. The teacher would look away, pretending not to notice. I became good at holding it in.

One boy in my class hadn't mastered that skill. He waved his hand desperately while the teacher kept ignoring him. Soon he started to squirm in his seat. When the puddle spread under his desk, the class burst out laughing. I looked down at my hands so he wouldn't think I was watching.

As the teacher escorted him to the office, my heart went out to him.

Sometimes alarms went off for air-raid drills. We crawled under our desks or lined up in the hallways with our backs against the cinder-block walls and our heads covered. The teachers' faces were so serious that it all felt authentic.

The only thing I remember clearly from those years is the third-grade reader, *Fun with Dick and Jane*. The books promised that childhood was fun.

At the end of the year, Mrs. Houlahan handed me a card that read,

"To a shy little girl. I will miss you."

~4~

Every Sunday, I attended catechism to prepare for my First Holy Communion. I sat quietly at my desk, scared to death of the ruler Sister Agnes kept slapping against her palm. She straightened her habit and cleared her throat. "Where is God?" she asked.

Obediently, we all answered in unison.

"God is Everywhere!"

We recited the *Our Father*, followed by the *Hail Mary* prayers that were drilled into our heads. After class, the nun led us to the church, single file, for Mass.

Our Lady of Guadalupe on 15th Avenue was thick with the air of holiness. It was a place with darkened halls and stained-glass windows. Leaving the outside world and entering this sanctuary, the scent of candles and incense mingled with the church's musty aroma.

As I dipped my finger into the holy water to make the sign of the cross, I felt protected by a higher power. I was assured this miracle liquid could wash away my problems.

The nuns guided the children to their seats and stood guard to keep order. Clad in their black robes and snug head coverings called a wimple, they seemed to have trouble turning their heads. Still, nothing ever escaped them.

I sat at the end of the first pew with most of my class behind me.

Everyone sang the hymns in the prayer book, but no sound came out when I opened my mouth.

The adults in front of me headed to the altar. Instinctively, I followed them.

We knelt and folded our hands in prayer as the priest moved down the row with a large gold cup, making the sign of the cross, just as we had practiced in class. The priest drew near. I closed my eyes and opened my mouth so he could place the wafer on my tongue. It was hard and dry, feeling like a piece of Styrofoam. As the wafer softened, it stuck to the roof of my mouth. I was too afraid to swallow or bite into it since the priest had told me it was the body of Christ.

Before I could sit down, one of the nuns yanked me out of the pew and dragged me outside. The blinding sun made me squint as I adjusted to the light. As my vision cleared, the nun's habit came into view. Then her face sharpened, and I saw the anger in Sister Agnes's eyes.

"You weren't supposed to receive communion until you completed your sacraments. You're going to Hell, young lady!"

I ran home sobbing.

My mother told me God would forgive me, but shame lingered long after.

Fear lived everywhere—in raised voices, in silence, even in holy places.

Two weeks after my incident with Sister Agnes, I developed a high fever. One day, everything went black. My appendix had ruptured. Unable to reach my father, my mother called my uncle. I remember his strong arms carrying me from the house and the bright lights of the hospital elevator before I slipped away again.

I awoke on a long table, surrounded by darkness, with a single light burning overhead. A mask covered my face. The smell of ether filled my lungs as I fought to move, kicking and swinging my arms, but I was powerless.

When I saw the light again, it was at the end of a long tunnel, pulling me toward it. When I turned, I saw a child in a hospital bed, with tubes rising and falling beside her. My parents stood nearby with a priest, their tears running down their faces.

The child was me.

I felt peaceful, almost weightless, but I didn't want my mother to cry. I resisted the light and returned to my body. It wasn't until I was an adult that I realized I had had an out-of-body experience.

I remember hushed voices and frightened faces as doctors spoke quietly by my bedside. My father argued with the doctors until the problem was corrected. After that, I began to improve. For months, a tube drained the infection, leaving a scar that looked like a second belly button.

The whole family came to see me. I basked in their attention. Games, dolls, and stuffed animals crowded my bed. People leaned in to hear me speak. For the first time, I felt surrounded by care.

After I arrived home, my parents treated me differently. Being sick had made me visible. Without realizing it, I came to believe that love arrived when someone needed saving.

When I finally made my First Communion, I walked up to the altar with my class and received the Host. I knelt in the pew and let the wafer melt on my tongue, feeling a holy glow as Jesus washed away my sins.

This time, I knew I wasn't going to hell.

After that day, the years seemed to move quickly, each marked by another ceremony, another expectation that I would behave properly and make my parents proud.

Before long, it was my Confirmation Day. I wore a beautiful white dress and a Jackie O. pillbox hat with a small bumblebee sewn into the veil. After the church ceremony, my dad took me to the park for pictures while my mom prepared for the party. Even on good days, I was careful not to upset him.

I reluctantly climbed into the passenger seat of his car, careful not to soil my new white gloves.

I looked like any other eleven-year-old girl, yet I didn't feel safe.

"Smile, Florence," my father instructed as he focused the camera on me.

I wanted to, but my mouth wouldn't.

"Florence," he yelled accusingly.

Hearing my name spoken like that made me cringe.

"Why won't you smile?"

Sensing my father's anger, I quickly thought of an excuse.

"I forgot to brush my teeth."

He shook his head in disgust and took me home, giving me a pass on the pictures.

After dinner, the adults shuffled cards at the table for a game of poker while the children played. From the living room, I could hear my father's jokes, his voice prompting howls of laughter from my aunts and uncles.

"She wouldn't smile because her teeth were dirty," he said. "Could you believe it?"

The room roared.

"Thank God her feet were clean, or she would've refused to walk."

Everyone laughed harder. I froze, wishing I could disappear, then laughed too, so no one would notice how much it hurt.

One day, my father decided I was too old for training wheels and removed them from my bike. He held the back wheel of the bike and told me to pedal. Suddenly, the bike felt lighter. I turned to look at my father, but he wasn't there. The wheels wobbled as I tried to stay in control. I thought he would be angry if I fell, so I didn't. I kept pedaling and pretended I wasn't afraid.

~5~

During the summer, we took the train to Coney Island. The beach was crowded, and the air smelled of salt and suntan lotion. Transistor radios blared music as we carefully stepped between towels spread across the sand.

The water was cold, but I went in and tried to keep from being tumbled by the waves. Before I realized how far I had gone, the shore was too far away. The more I tried to get back, the further I was carried. Panicked, I kicked and waved my arms until a man saw me struggling and pulled me in. After that, I didn't want to go into the water.

Instead, my brother and I built sandcastles by the shore. After a while, I looked up, but he was gone. I ran back to the blanket to tell my mom. She was frantic, and we searched up and down the beach for him. I hadn't told her that I was swept in a riptide and that I feared my brother had been too.

Hours later, when the crowds thinned, we found him playing by the fountain. The day was cut short, and we walked barefoot along the boardwalk to a bench so my mother could powder our feet and put our shoes on. We were lucky if we didn't get a splinter, but once I did. She had to take me to the first aid station, where they dug out the wood with a needle. It hurt.

Not long after, the neighborhood felt different. Boys began gathering in the park, their voices louder than before. Graffiti crept across the walls where children once played. The seesaws sat empty. Parents stopped bringing their younger kids. Even the old men who played cards under the trees disappeared. I still had to walk past the park every day on my way to school. I kept my eyes forward, counting my steps until I reached the corner.

Somewhere along the way, I learned to walk past the park without looking.

My parents noticed changes in the neighborhood and decided it was time to move.

They bought a two-bedroom pink colonial house on Elm Street in Long Island. It had a fenced-in yard, and the streets were clean—unlike in Brooklyn, where the street cleaners had to sweep every day.

The streets had names that matched the trees— Elm, Beech, Pine—as if everything belonged where it was supposed to be.

All the trees on our block were elms. For the first time, I felt a sense of order.

Inside our house, a staircase in the hall led up to a large attic with open walls and exposed insulation. There was only one light bulb hanging from the rafter. The kids slept on blankets spread across the wooden floor until my father could build the walls. My father used his carpentry skills to create two rooms. He installed electrical outlets powered by a single source, controlled by a switch at the bottom of the hall. It was hot that first summer and cold in the winter.

My brother had his own room, while I had to share with my sister. Our parents bought us matching bedroom furniture, including desks and chairs. Debra's chair broke. Whenever I went out, she'd swap it with mine. It became the first thing I checked when I entered the room. I wouldn't dare confront her about it. I was older, but she was stronger and meaner.

The neighborhood was very different from Brooklyn. Yards separated the houses, and people spoke with funny accents. I soon discovered that being from the city was a major obstacle. We were the city people who disrupted the suburban community's tranquil life.

The other girls on the block initially accepted me. One day, they invited me to see Cat Ballou. My mother gave me a small purse with enough money for a ticket and popcorn. We piled into the back of a station wagon. While the other girls were giddy and chatting on the way to the theater, I overheard their mothers whispering to each other.

"Why did you invite her?" one asked. "She's from the city."

"I didn't see the harm in it. She's just a little girl."

"Yes, but she may be a bad influence."

I sensed they were talking about me, but still, they invited me over to their houses to play with Barbie dolls. Although I was too old for dolls, I yearned to fit in, so I forced myself to be like them. But I couldn't keep up with what it took to stay in the game. I didn't have money for Barbie accessories—dresses, shoes, and purses.

Feeling their hostility, I secretly resented the fresh-faced little blond girls, especially the one who lived next door, Wendy.

She called me a city girl and said I didn't belong. My vision tunneled. I grabbed her hair and yanked. For a second, I didn't recognize myself. Strands slipped through my fingers.

After that, the other girls didn't play with me, but I didn't care. I hated dolls, anyway.

When school started at the end of the summer, I walked to school. Other kids walked in groups, but I was alone.

Every morning, I turned right onto the main road. If I had turned left, I would have reached the bar where my father hung out. I continued through the rural streets and over the bridge spanning the parkway, arriving at Albany Avenue Elementary School.

The school gave me the benefit of the doubt and placed me in a Regents class, a prerequisite for college entry. A young teacher came into our class at the end of each day. She was from France. French intrigued me, but all other subjects blurred together. Unable to keep up with the other kids, I fell behind, and the school administrator transferred me from the Regents class to a lower level. No more French!

Kids with vacant stares shoved past me in the hallway. I was a chubby little girl with a bad haircut and shabby clothes. They made me feel invisible unless I wanted to disappear.

An itchy rash bloomed on my chin. It crusted and scabbed. There was no hiding it. My mother took me to the doctor, who gave her calamine lotion, which only eased the itch. The rash crusted and formed a scab. There was no way to hide it. I had to go to school feeling self-conscious, ashamed, and dirty. It turned out I was allergic to—of all things—Ivory Soap.

~6~

Another school year began, and clothing was a luxury. I looked forward to ordering three outfits from the Sears catalog.

On the first day, the science teacher assigned me to a double desk with a partner.

I waited to see who would sit next to me.

When Dana dropped into the seat beside me, my stomach sank.

"What are you looking at?" she snapped, her eyes two sharpened spears.

Avoiding her gaze, I sat down, but I could still feel Dana's eyes on me.

The minute she spotted me, she verbally tore into me in front of everyone, starting with my shoes and working her way up.

"You wear the same thing every day," Dana said.

I tried to ignore her comments, but she was relentless.

Every day, Dana had something mean to say. It was going to be the worst year yet.

By January, my clothes were worn and faded. I noticed a rip on the left side of my purple paisley top and quickly covered it with my arm.

"Your shirt is ugly," she whispered.

Then she made fun of my pants. "You look like you're going to walk through a flood zone."

I hated her fresh face and those golden ringlets.

When I got home, I stared at myself in the full-length mirror on the bathroom door.

"Mom," I called out, then went downstairs to find her. "These pants are too short. You can see my ankles."

"Oh, they're fine," she replied absentmindedly.

"I don't want to wear them!"

My mother turned and stared at me. "What's wrong with you?"

"Well … there's this girl at school named Dana. She — she makes fun of me."

"So?" my mother said. "Make fun of her."

"I can't!"

"Why?"

"She's pretty and very popular. Everyone loves her, and she laughs when she calls me names."

"You need to speak up for yourself. Stand up to this girl. Say, 'I know you are, but what am I?' She'll get tired and give up. You'll see."

"I wish I were pretty like the other girls."

"Oh, Florence!" my mother laughed. "They may be pretty now, but you just wait. Girls like that usually end up looking like their mothers."

The next morning, following my mother's advice, I entered the classroom. My heart skipped a beat as Dana fixed on my pants. There was no avoiding it. I waited for my antagonist to pounce.

"You're so ugly," she said.

"I know you are, but what am I?" I recited the answer my mother had taught me.

Her eyes narrowed. "You're a moron!"

"I know you are, but what am I?"

I repeated the words because they were the only shield I had—even though they never stopped the arrows.

~7~

During the summer, my mother sent me to stay with my cousin Katie, who was a year older than me and an only child, at her country house on Long Island's North Shore. She inherited her German father's family traits, with long red hair flowing down her back, while mine was mousy brown and cut short.

Everything about her world felt different from mine. There were no sidewalks, only long roads lined with trees and the earthy scent of leaves and soil. At night, fireflies flickered over the grass like tiny neon lights, and the crickets chirped so loudly that they sometimes kept me awake. Other nights, their steady chorus comforted me.

Katie moved through that world as if she owned it. She had plenty of friends and seemed good at everything. Trophies crowded her room, proof of her talents.

I tried to imagine what it felt like to be celebrated.

My aunt Anna loved dressing us alike. My favorite outfit was a short set with the four Beatles across the front, each with black yarn hair.

Sometimes my uncle took us swimming at Head of the Harbor on Long Island Sound. We'd drive down a long, tree-shaded road and stop first at the General Store for candy sticks of every flavor. I loved those outings.

The summer he bought her a pony, the difference between us felt impossible to miss. We spent every day at the stables. Katie rode while I stood by the fence, watching, pretending that I didn't mind being the girl on the outside looking in. I told myself it was enough just to be there.

My mother admired Katie. She praised her straight A's and helpfulness. When Katie visited our house, she would jump up after dinner to wash the dishes.

"Oh, what a good girl," my mother would say.

I wanted that kind of approval and tried to imitate my cousin, but whatever came naturally to her seemed to slip through my fingers.

In fifth grade, I won the Best Character award. It mattered to me, but no one seemed to notice.

Although I didn't do well academically, I always got high marks on projects — with a little help from my father.

If I had a school assignment, he would eagerly offer to help.

Once, he built a covered wagon that was the envy of my classmates.

"How did you make this?" the teacher asked. She suspected I hadn't made it, but she still displayed it in the glass case in the school hallway for everyone to see.

I felt like a fraud, but kept the secret to myself.

In sixth grade, my father built a space project. The other kids followed and laughed as I carried it to my classroom.

"It's nothing but a box with a hole," they said.

I placed it on the teacher's desk and plugged the cord into the wall outlet. Everyone gathered around to see what it was. When they looked inside, a galaxy illuminated.

A small light set inside a flying saucer that hung from a string illuminated fluorescent stars and drawings of planets and comets shooting across a black construction-paper background.

My father waited for me to come home from school at the end of the day. The excited look on his face reminded me of a small boy on Christmas. He kept asking me to tell him again how much everyone loved it.

I told the story the way he wanted to hear it, again and again.

~8~

My mother's life as a homemaker looked pleasant from the outside — a little shopping, afternoon soap operas, and regular trips to the beauty salon. She was beautiful, her auburn hair swept into an elegant updo, a curly hairpiece giving her the look of a Greek goddess. But her beauty could not hide her sadness. She never seemed happy as a wife or a mother.

She described my father as an ogre, shaking her head at the kitchen table as smoke curled from her cigarette.

As a young woman, she loved to sing and dreamed of performing on Broadway. She came close. A producer once handed her his card and told her to return when she turned eighteen. Then she met my father, and the dream quietly faded.

Unhappy with her life, my mother found an escape in Bingo. She spent her money and time in a smoke-filled auditorium night after night.

Occasionally, my mother took me along. It made me feel special. Like, there was no one else in the world but us. She'd buy me a hot dog or a slice of pizza, hand me a red dot marker and a single bingo card, and keep one eye on her own.

I prayed I would win the jackpot so I could give her the money and make her happy, but I never won.

As my mother washed the dishes after dinner, she

whispered, "Florence, do you mind if I go to bingo at the church tonight? Your father's acting up, and I need to get out for a few hours."

Afraid of alienating her, I smiled and told her I understood.

"You're the only one who understands," she said.

I didn't yet know how to refuse. Saying yes felt safer than risking her disappointment.

After she left, the house felt different. I hated being left alone with my father. Her absence often made him drink.

Once she was gone, Dad called me from my bedroom. I couldn't avoid him. He'd shut off the switch in the hall.

The lights upstairs went dark. I knew he wanted me to come down. I stood there a moment, listening, before slinking down the stairs.

He was still in his work uniform. The bottle of Scotch on the dining room table told me he had already begun drinking.

I obediently took a seat.

"Your mother is no good!" he said, his eyes blazing. He knocked back another shot and searched my face for a reaction.

"All she cares about is your aunt and her daughter," he continued.

I avoided his eyes as he hit upon my own suspicions.

He waited for me to agree, but all I could do was stare out the sliding glass doors into the yard, my eyes fixed on the leaves moving in the trees or the birds perched on the clothesline.

"She doesn't love me. She doesn't even want to have sex."

At thirteen years old, I didn't understand what he meant.

"Maybe you could talk to her," I said, compelled to keep the peace. But my efforts felt futile.

"Let me tell you something! Your mother doesn't care about me or you."

He waited for me to say something else, but I sat very still, afraid that disagreeing would make things worse.

My father, the youngest of three brothers, was a mama's boy. He grew into a good-looking man with dark, curly hair and soulful brown eyes. His family had emigrated from Naples to Manhattan's Little Italy, and he was crushed when his mother died young.

He lived mostly on the margins of my life. I only glimpsed who he really was when he wasn't angry or drunk.

My parents' relationship had always been unstable. Even at the dinner table, there was fighting. Food was scarce, and my siblings and I argued over who had the most peas.

My father blamed my mother for overspending on bingo, and my mother blamed him for not earning enough to buy more food. No one blamed the drinking.

They went to marriage counseling for a while, and things calmed down. For a while, our house felt almost normal. My father stopped going to the bar. The fighting stopped long enough for my mother to become pregnant again.

While my mother was in the hospital giving birth, I was responsible for getting my sister Debra off to school. I enjoyed the caregiving role and dug out our old Singer sewing machine.

Using fabric my aunt had given me from the textile factory where she worked, I sewed a little red cape.

She was thrilled and rushed to leave for school. Just as she stepped out the door, I noticed a loose thread.

"Wait, Debra. I have to cut that thread."

I ran downstairs for scissors and tumbled down the entire flight. Limping back up the stairs, I cut the loose thread and sent her off to school.

My father's sobriety lasted only until Carol was born. His drinking slowly wore my mother down, and her unhappiness settled over the house like a fog.

She often threatened to leave him, but never did.

I didn't understand why she stayed. I only knew she stayed. Loving her meant not making things harder.

My mother didn't like messes. When she went into "cleaning mode," nothing was safe — not drawings, not toys, not anything else we cared about.

So when she went out, I cleaned the house from top to bottom, hoping she would notice when she returned.

She didn't.

One Friday morning, I walked into the kitchen just as my mother opened a can of tuna and two small cans of eggplant caponata.

I knew my Aunt Anna would arrive any minute, so I lingered. I told my mother my stomach hurt, hoping she would let me stay home, but she waved me off, certain I was trying to avoid school. A fresh, buttered poppy-seed roll didn't make up for the little party I knew I would miss.

At school, boys stared as I walked by, making me painfully aware that my body had developed earlier than the other girls in my class.

Everything seemed to be changing, though I didn't yet realize some of those changes were happening to me.

The cramps followed me all morning. When I went to the girls' bathroom, I noticed blood in my panties. Panic rose in my chest. I ran to the nurse's office.

She smiled as if nothing were wrong and handed me a blue-and-white box. I recognized the label from the box under our sink at home. Inside was a pad attached to a web of straps that fastened around my waist. She showed me how to use it, then had me lie down on a cot behind a thin curtain before calling my mother.

My mother arrived a few minutes later with Aunt Anna beside her.

"You're a woman now," my aunt said. "How does it feel?"

I nodded, pretending I understood what it meant.

The heaviness between my legs made me walk carefully. We went home, and I ate lunch with them at the kitchen table, shifting in my chair while they talked as if something important had happened.

~9~

I became friends with Josephine through a neighbor down the street. Josie was sweet, kind, and easygoing. Living with two older sisters gave her a sense of security I had never experienced. Being around them was the closest thing I knew to feeling normal.

I walked to her bus stop every morning to catch the school bus. She was in honor-roll classes, while I was placed in the lowest general-level class. My classes felt more like babysitting than learning. The work was easy. Just showing up guaranteed a passing grade. At the end of the day, we rode the bus home together.

We'd rush up to her bedroom and lock the door. Josie's room was a magical place. Perfume and face powder hung in the air like a display at a department store cosmetics counter. Eyeliners, lipsticks, and powder compacts cluttered her vanity. Josie shared the room with her older sister, Ellen, who sometimes sent us to the deli to buy cigarettes for her. She gave each of us a quarter to run the errand. Back then, candy cost a nickel, so we stocked up on red licorice whips and Three Musketeer bars. Ellen stayed in her room, chain-smoking the whole pack while we sat under a tree in the backyard, eating our treats.

Josie had much less freedom than I did. She had to come home from school every day and wasn't allowed outside after dark. When I slept over, Ellen stayed with their other sister, Kristi, and I slept in Josie's bed. We listened to music and smoked cigarettes, blowing the smoke out the window. Sometimes we put on makeup at her vanity mirror, then climbed out the window to wander the neighborhood streets, singing and laughing. We stayed up all night playing card games — Spit, Crazy Eights, and War.

Josie spent the night at my house whenever we wanted to hang out with the other kids at the local deli. My mother was preoccupied and didn't pay much attention to us, so we came and went as we pleased. I thought her mother was too strict.

Once, I ran away from home and hid in Josie's bedroom closet. She sneaked some of her Polish mother's special potato pancakes to me, which she swore were delicious. The food looked foreign to me, but I ate it anyway so I wouldn't hurt her feelings. After one bite, I wondered what all the fuss was about. We thought her parents didn't know I was there, but the missing food gave us away. Her mother insisted that I go home. No one noticed I'd been gone as I climbed the stairs to my room.

The kids at the back of the bus didn't bother Josie. They said she looked wholesome. Instead, they picked on me. It felt like I was wearing a sign on my back that said *Kick Me*. Maybe it was my Mediterranean skin tone. Most of the other girls had fair skin, blonde hair, or blue eyes. They looked squeaky clean. The word *wholesome* started to grate on me.

Not long after, a new family moved to town. They were Italian, and the two older boys were wild. The younger one, Salvatore, immediately took a dislike to me and started a rumor that I was a tramp. The news spread quickly. How do you fight something like that? I was just turning sixteen and hadn't even had my first boyfriend.

At my school, ruining a girl's reputation was practically a sport. All it took was accusing a girl of being a tramp, and her entire world changed. Girls shunned me, while boys flocked around, thinking I was loose.

I couldn't hang out at the deli anymore. Whenever Salvatore was there, I felt the threat of another verbal attack. He'd cut me down if I dared to stand up for myself.

The rumor eventually reached Josie's oldest sister, Kristi, who insisted that Josie shouldn't hang around with me anymore. We secretly phoned each other during the summer, but it wasn't the same.

Again, I sought my mother's help. She gave me a small gold cross to wear. I didn't believe it would protect me, yet I never took it off. It was proof she cared.

I loved her deeply, but closeness never lasted. One moment, she was attentive; the next, she pulled away. I learned to adapt to her moods, craving approval that felt like candy—sweet but never enough.

On the way home from school, a group of girls behind me talked and laughed. Hearing Dana's voice, I trembled. I had a terrible feeling that something was about to happen, so I quickened my pace.

"Look at her hair," a voice said.

The other girls laughed. "Pull it!"

Hearing her laugh, I braced myself.

No, wait! Dana wasn't laughing. She was crying!

"Leave me alone!" she sobbed.

"Leave me alooone," another girl mocked. There was a scuffle. Cautiously, I turned to look over my shoulder. Dana was on the ground. A trickle of blood ran down her cheek, mingling with her tears.

"Stop," I yelled, my voice cracking. All eyes turned to me.

"What are you going to do about it?" the toughest girl said. She shoved me back, but I didn't fall. My heart pounded as she came at me again. This time, I pushed her back. Now I was the target.

"You shouldn't have done that," the girl threatened, raising her fist. Sensing a fight was about to begin, the other girls cheered. Before she could strike, I grabbed her long brown hair. I yanked harder each time she hit me until she screamed for me to let go. But it was too late for that! I pulled and twisted with pent-up anger. Finally, she stopped swinging, and I let go. I looked down at my still-clenched fist. Clumps of brown hair were entangled between my fingers.

Dana's eyes opened wide with surprise.

When I approached my desk the next day, Dana opened her mouth to say something mean, but then stopped. She had no more words of ridicule.

After that, something changed between us. We started making small talk and became friends.

Dana invited me to her house after school, and I rode home on her bus. I was amazed that her family was even more impoverished than mine. They were on welfare, and she lived in a small house with two brothers and three sisters. Her older brother had a car parked in the driveway. It didn't run, but it was a hangout for him and his friends.

Sometimes he let us sit in his car. Eventually, he became my first boyfriend, and we spent hours making out in the backseat.

Dana and I started having lunch together. The other kids began to take notice. One of the boys in the lunchroom remarked that I wasn't as wholesome-looking as Dana. I suspected it was because she looked like the proverbial girl next door. My dark hair might have given me a more sinister appearance.

Josie, Dana, and I became best friends. Now we were three girls. All at once, Long Island didn't seem so bad.

One day, my friend Dana told me she had a surprise for me. I rode the bus home with her. We had the house to ourselves. Dana reached under her mattress and pulled out a pack of cigarettes. She handed me one and struck a match. After lighting her cigarette, she held it up for me to light mine.

Pretending to inhale, I took a drag, held it briefly, then exhaled.

"Where's your brother?" I asked.

"Oh, he's getting high with his friends. He won't bother us." Dana jumped up and rummaged through her dresser.

She gave me a devious smile and held up a plastic bag.

"I managed to sneak some of his weed while he wasn't looking."

My eyes widened. "You smoke pot?"

"Sure, everyone who's the slightest bit cool smokes pot. You're going to love it!" Dana opened the bag, pinched some of the contents between her fingers, and then laid them on a small white sheet of paper.

"It looks like oregano."

Dana laughed. "You're so naïve!" She nimbly rolled the leaves into a tight cylinder and held it up to admire her handiwork. "Another perfect joint!"

Dana struck another match and lit the joint. She sucked in the smoke, held her breath for a moment, then coughed. Smoke blew out of her mouth.

"Are you all right?"

"Yeah, stupid, you're supposed to cough," she said, handing it to me. "It's your turn."

Hesitantly, I puffed on the joint, letting some of the smoke touch my throat before blowing it out.

"Hold it in longer," she insisted.

I took a puff and held my breath until my lungs felt like they would burst. "I don't feel anything," I said.

"Sometimes you have to do it for a while, but when it hits you, you'll know it and love it."

We continued to take turns smoking the joint, and, as Dana said, the feeling came on suddenly. I felt like I was floating. By the time I went home, I was smoking like a pro, inhaling both cigarettes *and* pot.

My appearance began to change. I started wearing jeans and t-shirts, some of which featured peace signs on the front. Jeans became cool in tenth grade. They shielded girls from low-income families from the fashion advantages of the popular girls. Feeling creative, I lined each pant leg with metal studs from the knee to the hem.

We hung out at the Village Green in Farmingdale, a popular spot where people gathered to listen to live music and enjoy recreational activities.

One day at school, Dana looked upset.

"My parents found my pot stash. I'm in serious trouble."

"What did you tell them?"

Dana laughed. "They think you're a pusher."

Dana's fresh-faced innocence protected her. Wholesome. That's what she was.

Soon, Dana was swallowing little red Seconals as if they were Pez candies. I knew taking drugs was wrong, but I feared losing her friendship if I refused to go along.

One night at Jones Beach, we gathered around a campfire. I ate a few pills and passed out. My friends propped me up against the railing of my parents' house in the middle of the night, rang the doorbell, then jumped in the car and took off.

"She's on goofballs!" My father screamed, making my mother cry.

What hurt most was the look on my mother's face—surprise, followed by disappointment.

For a moment, I felt like the little girl crouched on the backseat floor again.

Part Two

Identity

My cousin Lee graduated one year before me. She was going to Miami University in her new yellow Volkswagen Bug, a car I found hideous, but I still envied her independence. While she was having adventures in sunny Florida, I was finishing my last year of high school.

Throughout my academic life, I struggled with taking tests. When everything around me was calm, the chaos in my head quieted. My brain shut down the moment I encountered a stressful situation. I couldn't even fill in the correct bubble on a multiple-choice sheet.

My school advisor urged me to drop math and science. He said I wasn't college material.

They shoved me into Basic English and electives like Home Economics and record-keeping.

At first, I thought it was great. No homework, no pressure, just empty hours waiting for the bell to ring.

Nothing was expected, and nothing was achieved.

Between classes, students stood outside the wings, smoking cigarettes. By then, I was smoking a pack a day with my friends. Sometimes, I cut class and hung out in the *Commons*, a large area where students congregated when they weren't in class.

All my classes were in the morning. The last was P.E., which I often cut to go home for lunch.

No one cared except for one teacher, Mr. Lieberman, the record-keeping instructor. When he saw me in the hall with a friend, he stopped me and lectured me about skipping class. Somehow, he recognized my potential.

"You're wasting your potential," he said. "You could be great at accounting if you put your mind to it."

Accounting?

I liked numbers. Maybe that was something I could actually be good at. For the first time, college didn't feel like someone else's dream. I asked the school counselor for some brochures and couldn't wait to tell my father.

His face twisted. "I don't have money for college," he said.

Just like that, the dream collapsed.

I put it aside and accepted that I would never go to college. The way I saw it, my only option was to get married.

So, I searched for my prince charming. I kissed one frog after another. No prince appeared.

~2~

While I was waiting for my life to start, my uncle used some connections to get me a job at the aerospace company where he worked.

I drove through the gates and stopped at the guard's station.

"My name is Florence St. John. It's my first day."

He smiled. "You'll need a badge." He handed me a small placard with my name on it. "This badge is only temporary. Please go to the administration office to get your picture taken. They'll give you the real one."

I approached the front desk in the lobby and showed my temporary badge. The receptionist looked at me through heavily lined eyes and false lashes. Her long red fingernails tapped on the computer.

"Take a seat. I'll call someone to escort you to your department.

Soon, a girl around my age walked out through the double doors.

"Hi, I'm Joanne," she said. "I'm the head Dippy Girl."

"Dippy Girl?"

She laughed. "That's what they call us. It stands for data input processing."

Leaving the lobby behind, I followed her through the same double doors into a different world. Jet fuel lingered in the air as we moved through the dimly lit tunnels of the plant. My mind wandered as I took in the sights and sounds. It was a far cry from being a housewife, and I hoped I wasn't in over my head.

The roar of a fighter jet shook the building from a distant hangar. It grew louder as we turned a corner, and I caught sight of an F-14 across the complex. It was magnificent!

Drills and heavy machinery drowned out our conversation as we entered the first department. Rows of workbenches filled the space. It reminded me of a lab class I took in school. At each bench, men worked with metal or electronic boards. Some were young, but most were old enough to be my father. There were no women.

"Hey! We have a new Dippy Girl," one of the workers yelled.

Everyone looked up and smiled as Joanne led me to a computer. Next to it was a cart filled with various plane parts wrapped in plastic sheathing. Each label had a code, and I had to input each part number into the computer.

"The red cart is for incoming parts, and the blue cart is for outgoing," she explained. "You can stay here today. I'll train you in the other departments when you get the hang of it. Come to the ladies' room if you run out of work." Joanne laughed. "That's where the data processing girls hang out and talk about company office politics. You know—who's going out with whom or getting a promotion?"

Later, I stopped by the ladies' room. Three girls were already there. They glanced up when I walked in, then went back to talking about Rudy's new mistress.

"She isn't very pretty," one girl said. "I don't know what Rudy sees in her."

Joanne bounced into the room. "Hi, Florence! I'm glad you decided to join us."

The other girls warmed up a little, but I had no intention of becoming part of Joanne's little gossip circle. Petty talk had never interested me. I had seen the damage gossip could do in high school.

But the work itself suited me.

The machines didn't judge.

The parts had numbers, and the numbers made sense.

For the first time in a long while, I felt useful. That feeling kept me coming back every morning.

~3~

I loved working at Frontier Aerospace. I was the only female in my department, and the older guys treated me like a daughter. Sal, the manager, would bring me a cup of coffee with cream every morning, but he always forgot the sugar. I said nothing for fear of insulting him and learned to like it that way. He was a quiet man. Everyone loved him because he was generous with praise and rewarded his employees. Wednesdays were golf days, and he took a few workers out to play. Once, he even took me. The other players wondered why I was allowed to tag along. I wasn't sure either, but I was excited to spend the day on the golf course for full pay. Sometimes, he even took me out to lunch. It made me feel important. He slowly gained my trust, and it became a ritual.

As Sal moved up the corporate ladder, he promoted me with him—I became the administrative secretary with higher pay, more status, and more privileges. I had more power than my young brain could conceive.

One day, after lunch, he suggested we go to the park. I didn't think much of it because Sal was my protector, advisor, and champion.

It was fall, my favorite time of year. The leaves gently floated to the ground, their colors a blend of purple, gold, and red. We sat in his car, waiting for a deer to emerge from the thick brush. Before we left, Sal pulled me to him and kissed me on the mouth.

In that moment, I understood the deer differently—quiet, watchful, unaware that danger was already standing beside it. Sal had called the other managers piranhas for years, and he turned out to be just like them.

Manipulated by a man who exploited my vulnerability, I felt trapped. No one could rescue me. One day, an opening in the computer department came up, so I took it. I was free.

But freedom didn't bring the clarity I expected. I still didn't know who I was or where I belonged.

~4~

Born under the fire sign of Leo, I wanted to believe in the zodiac hype—confident, ambitious, generous, loyal, and encouraging. In truth, I struggled to understand who I was. I longed for a place where I belonged.

I didn't realize back then that many kids grew up in families that boosted their confidence and expected them to succeed. My shyness made me seem distant and uninterested. I drifted from year to year, trying to connect with someone, anyone.

My mother used to say I'd know when love arrived, but I had long given up the myth that someday my prince would come.

I wasn't looking for a relationship, but there he was — an old neighbor.

He pulled up in front of my house and got off his motorcycle. Wearing shabby clothes, he looked almost ready to be homeless. His long hair hung down from his ski cap. Nothing about him appealed to me. At first, I pretended that I wasn't home, but he kept showing up at my door.

Edward was kind in an earthy, uncomplicated way. I was lonely, so we became friends.

We used to drive around in my car exploring nature preserves and hiking trails. He shared his botanical knowledge, and before winter ended, he had grown on me like moss on the north side of a tree.

A few months later, I sat down at the kitchen table while my mother washed the dishes in the sink.

"Are you all right, Florence? You look a little pale."

"Yes… uh… no." Tears welled in my eyes. "Mom, I need to talk to you about something."

Her smile faded. "What's wrong?"

"Edward asked me to marry him," I blurted.

Her eyes widened a bit. "Oh. And what did you say?"

"I haven't given him an answer yet. I'm not sure if I love him."

She reached across the table and placed her hand on mine. "Love is complicated. It's not always straightforward, especially when you're young. You're only twenty-two. You have plenty of time. There's no need to rush into marriage if you're unsure."

I stared at my trembling hands.

"Mom," I said, my voice breaking. "I... I'm pregnant."

The room went still.

She blinked in shock, then slowly sank into the nearest chair.

"Pregnant?" she repeated, the word hanging in the air between us. "Are you sure?"

I nodded, my eyes fixed on the floor.

She sighed. "You're so young," she said, her voice strained with worry. "This isn't the life I wanted for you."

I wasn't sure it was the life I wanted either.

Part Three

When I announced my pregnancy, Edward immediately asked me to marry him. The last thing I expected was for him to find a job in Houston.

Six months pregnant, I said goodbye to my mother. I had never lived so far from home.

Houston was suffocatingly hot—a sticky, relentless heat I had never experienced back in New York. Each doctor's appointment reminded me I would be delivering my baby among strangers. The baby moved and stretched inside me. It was the only part of pregnancy that felt certain.

By nine months, I was about to have my own baby—someone I could nurture and pour all my love into.

A week went by, and there was still no sign of labor. The doctor said the due date might have been miscalculated or that the first baby often takes longer to arrive.

I practiced the breathing techniques I had learned in Lamaze class. Hours passed, and my baby still refused to be born.

Then the monitor started beeping loudly, and I began to feel dizzy.

"Fetal distress," the nurse shouted. "Call the doctor, stat!"

Her voice faded as the room went dark. For a moment, the hospital lights above me seemed oddly familiar.

When I opened my eyes, I found myself alone in a hospital bed. I called for the nurse.

"Where's my baby?"

"She's in the nursery and doing fine," she said gently. "Don't worry."

A few minutes later, she placed a perfect baby girl in my arms.

She helped position Annmarie at my breast while I waited to feel the bliss of bonding they had promised in Lamaze class. Annmarie opened her mouth and turned her head, trying to latch onto my nipple, but after a moment she grew frustrated and began to cry.

"Don't panic," the nurse said. "Sometimes it takes a little time."

Even though I fed Annmarie every hour, she was still hungry. I didn't have enough milk.

"I guess I'll bring you some formula for now," the nurse said. "But breast milk is best, so keep trying."

I felt like a failure.

Living in an unfamiliar place with no one to support me as a new mother, I did my best, but hearing my baby cry made me anxious. I had assumed maternal instinct would come naturally. Instead, I felt unsure of everything.

Annmarie was colicky right from the moment we brought her home. No matter what I did, she cried.

After a month, I gave up and bought infant formula. For the first time, Annmarie seemed full and satisfied. My guilt about breastfeeding started to decrease, but the pressure to do everything perfectly kept me constantly on edge.

I went to the pediatrician every time she sneezed and followed his advice carefully. When he said she wasn't gaining enough weight, I started her on solid foods. Annmarie tolerated cereal and fruit but refused the baby food meats. I bought a feeder with a rubber nipple designed to help babies swallow pureed food.

Her face scrunched up the moment she realized it wasn't milk.

Nothing I did seemed right. I kept telling myself it would get easier.

Within the year, I was pregnant again. Annmarie was only eighteen months old — still a baby herself.

The months that followed passed in a blur of diapers, bottles, and exhaustion.

~2~

It was Christmas, and I was nearing the end of my ninth month. In the South, some mothers even put Coca-Cola in their babies' bottles. I thought that was a terrible practice, so I gave her Tang instead. It was loaded with vitamin C, and I believed it was more nutritious than Coke.

During a routine exam, the doctor noticed decay behind her front teeth. She had "bottle-rot," which was common among babies who went to bed with a bottle. Honestly, I saw nothing wrong with using a bottle at bedtime. I later learned this was the worst thing you could do. I had damaged my baby's teeth! Wanting to do what was best for my child, I took her to a pediatric dentist.

Annmarie cried as they led her away, but their policy was not to allow the parent to be present. Against my better judgment, I let them take her to the examination room while I paced around the waiting area. I had to find a restroom, so I walked down the hall. My ears picked up the familiar cry of a child. Annmarie! She was crying on the other side of the wall. Her screams chilled me to the bone. I wanted to burst through the door and make them stop, but I sat helplessly on a bench in the hall. We were both red-eyed with tears when she finally came out of the examination room. I hugged her and apologized.

The dentist told us she needed root canals and silver caps on her teeth. He explained that he had to restrain her in a sheet-like papoose cradle, but would give her a mild sedative so she would stay still.

As far as I could tell, Annmarie didn't complain of any pain from her teeth. The only memory I had as a child related to teeth was having them pulled out of my mouth one by one by the time I was five. Then, if you had a cavity, the tooth was removed. Replacement teeth, a permanent set, would come in later.

The whole procedure shocked me—restraining a baby and drilling into her teeth with only a mild sedative. An adult might be able to express discomfort, but all a baby can do is cry and endure the pain. It's inhumane.

After doing more research, I canceled the appointment. That should have been the end, but the doctor threatened to call child protective services, claiming that my husband and I neglected my daughter's health.

Gathering my resources, I contacted other dentists for a second opinion, but I soon realized that doctors weren't comfortable contradicting each other. I started calling dentists in New York. Most did not agree about performing root canals on an eighteen-month-old, but they couldn't support my decision since they had not examined my child. After exploring every option to oppose the procedure, my husband and I surrendered.

On the day of the appointment, I was a wreck. The image of my screaming, terrified daughter pinned to a chair for hours while the dentist worked in her mouth made me sick to my stomach.

My baby had eight root canals—four in the front, two in the upper back, and two in the lower back teeth.

When she stepped out of the dentist's office, I barely recognized her. Annmarie's eyes were swollen and red, and her mouth was filled with bloody, silver teeth. Her clothes and hair reeked of vomit. She looked exhausted and struggled to keep her eyes open. But when she managed to do so, confusion and accusation flickered in her gaze, as if she wanted to ask, "Why did you let them do this to me, Mommy?"

It felt as if I had broken a fundamental trust. The same trust that every child places in their mother to protect them.

According to psychologist Erik Erikson, one of a child's first lessons is trust—the belief that those who care for them will keep them safe.

Holding Annmarie that day, I questioned whether I had broken that trust.

As the days passed, Annmarie's appetite waned. She couldn't chew her food, and I watched her transform from a healthy, chubby-cheeked, outgoing baby into a thin, sickly, shy child. The dentist assured me it would pass, but he was wrong. Some caps fell out. Refusing to return to the dentist who had hurt her, I found another who agreed to use general anesthesia this time, and he allowed me to stay with her. Afterward, her trust in me and the outside world seemed to vanish. The ordeal might have been over, but she would wake up with night terrors every night if she got tangled in her sheets, which continued into her teens.

Some experts believe that early trauma can impact a child's developing brain.

Maybe the dental procedure affected something in her brain. [1]

I hadn't realized the psychological scars from her dental work yet. Annmarie stopped smiling and looked sad in a way I knew all too well. But I held onto hope that her life would be different from mine. Thin and frail, she was afraid of people, including other kids. They teased her, calling her "metal mouth.

She started to withdraw, and feeling uncomfortable with the social silence, I felt compelled to step in.

---

[1] Traumatic Stress Effects on the Brain - J. Douglas Bremner, M.D.

"What's your name, little girl?"
Silence.
"Her name is Annmarie."
"How old are you?"
Silence.
"She's three... four... five," I answered.

~3~

During an Easter egg hunt at preschool, the kids hurried around searching for eggs, but Annmarie stayed in the middle of the schoolyard. Instead of competing with the other children, she simply gave up. The teachers assured me that nothing was wrong. She was just a quiet, well-behaved kid, but I knew better.

Annmarie had low self-esteem. I recognized it immediately because I had seen it in the women in my family — and in myself.

After my second child was born, I dedicated myself entirely to home and family. I told myself that being a full-time mother would finally bring me fulfillment. I chose the stay-at-home mom role I believed would satisfy me and hid behind my marriage from the pressures of the outside world.

Playing Suzy Homemaker, all I had to do was please my husband and children — a little of cooking, cleaning, gardening, and watching soap operas like my mother.

My mother wasn't there for me — I would be there for my children. Thinking I could make up for everything I missed in my childhood, I took on the role of Supermom — able to leap social problems in a single bound.

When we moved into our new house in Georgia, I was happy that the girl across the street was Annmarie's age. Kimmy was outgoing and confident. I hoped they would become best friends and grow up together.

Kimmy took ballet classes. I remembered wanting to take dance when I was her age. I begged my father for the three dollars needed for dance lessons with a woman who had previously danced with the Rockettes at Radio City Music Hall. He pointed out that I would need ballet slippers and a leotard and said he couldn't afford them.

I signed Annmarie up, hoping it would boost her confidence. But Annmarie just stood off to the side, watching the other girls' plié and twirl.

After that, Kimmy seemed to avoid her. Annmarie wasn't invited when Kimmy had other friends over to hang out.

Then one day, I heard a string of notes that sounded like a familiar song. Annmarie had received a small electronic keyboard for Christmas and figured out the melody from a Disney movie we had watched just a few days before.

I thought about Judy, a retired piano teacher who lived across the hollow in a small log cabin. She had a piano and had agreed to give Annmarie lessons. I walked my daughter through the woods to Judy's house and looked forward to Annmarie's growing talent.

She was doing well on the small keyboard, but I felt she needed something better. So, I bought her a real piano. It was a black laminate upright and a bit expensive, but Edward agreed.

Annmarie was worth it.

~4~

Motherhood gave me purpose, but it was a fragile kind of confidence — one that relied on proving my worth.

I spent my days cooking, cleaning, caring for babies, and trying to earn my place by being perfect.

I appeared confident. But it was an illusion.

I was re-enacting my mother's life — soap operas and all — while my emotions roiled beneath the surface like a storm. I felt myself slipping away. Without a life of my own, I clung to anything that made me feel needed.

I wasn't happy, but I couldn't admit I'd chosen the wrong life. I missed my family on Long Island.

Holidays were the hardest. We decorated cookies — bunnies for Easter, pumpkins for Halloween, turkeys for Thanksgiving, Santas for Christmas. Frosting on small fingers, sprinkles everywhere. Christmas was the toughest. As long as I didn't hear the music, I could cope. But the first jingle of a carol — just one line — could take my breath away. I'd go quiet, then force my smile back on my face and keep going, hoping the holiday would pass quickly.

Not long after, the past caught up with me. After thirty-three years of fighting, my parents' marriage finally ended.

~5~

Mom moved into my guest room while she looked for a place of her own.

At first, I was happy to have her. I tried to blend my extended family into my household, but within a month, the turmoil I had grown up with resurfaced.

I wanted to do right by my children, but Mom treated it as a competition. She challenged everything I did. Maybe it threatened her self-esteem, or maybe she viewed it as criticism of her own mothering.

She made me feel like I was doing something wrong. "Your daughter doesn't want to play the piano," she pointed out. "Why are you forcing her?"

"She needs to try different activities. How else will she discover what she's good at?"

"I never made you do activities."

"Yes, I know... and I wish you had."

"You never showed interest in anything. Besides, I was barely getting by on the little money your father gave me. I did the best I could. You don't understand how hard my life was. Your father was always at the bar."

"I know, I remember, Mom."

"Making her take lessons won't change anything. You'll see. Kids never appreciate what we do for them."

Without her approval, I wavered for a moment. Maybe she was reacting to her own guilt for not giving her children those opportunities.

If I'm a good mother, she might feel like a bad one. I couldn't be angry, but I also couldn't accept her challenge. She only valued my opinions when they supported her emotionally. I knew this, but I pushed my anger down.

Although I needed my mother, living together wasn't working for either of us.

Meanwhile, my Aunt Anna bought a townhouse in Florida to live closer to her daughter. She gushed about the Florida sunshine and the neat community. It must have triggered jealousy in my mother. Or maybe she simply felt the tension between us. She decided to move to Florida. My aunt found her a townhouse, and my mother bought it sight unseen.

Devastated, I forced a smile and told my mother I understood. But the voice inside my head whispered that I still wasn't good enough.

After she left, a quiet emptiness settled over the house.

Part Four

I believed that mother-daughter love was different from any other kind of love—an unspoken bond of nurturing that nothing could break. Even as an adult, I still reached for my mother's approval.

We spoke every day. I kept trying to find ways to make her happy—small gestures, gifts, shared plans. Sometimes they landed well; sometimes they didn't. What stayed with me wasn't disappointment so much as confusion. I never quite understood why doing something loving so often left me feeling inadequate.

My mother loved her life in Florida, but my sister Carol never seemed to settle into it as we had hoped. She was gentle and sweet, like the glaze on a Krispy-Kreme doughnut, but beneath that softness, she often appeared overwhelmed by life.

Gambling became my mother's obsession. While I avoided risk, she was drawn to it, convinced that luck might finally turn her way. It started harmlessly enough—Bingo, small bets, the thrill of possibility—but over time, she spent her money at OTB and went on gambling cruises.

I seldom challenged her. Silence seemed easier than confrontation.

When my sister Carol called to say our mother was "talking funny," a cold heaviness settled in my stomach. She put Mom on the phone.

"Mom? Are you all right?" I asked.

She mumbled, repeating the same words until Carol came back on the line, her voice shaking.

"I don't know what's wrong with her," she cried.

"I think she's having a stroke. Get her to the hospital."

"She's refusing. I don't know what to do."

I could sense the panic beneath her words and knew our mother was being stubborn, refusing help as she always had.

"If she won't go willingly, call an ambulance."

"I can't," Carol said. "She'll get mad at me."

"Carol, she needs help."

I understood her fear, but this was bigger than loyalty or anger.

The hospital confirmed it was a stroke. Damage to the left side of her brain caused her speech to become slurred and left her body weakened. Soon, we gathered at her bedside — me, Carol, and Debra. Standing around her bed, old tensions seemed to fade away. Whatever history existed between us, love remained.

The woman who always appeared strong and unmoving now looked small and frightened, as if someone had unplugged her from the power source that kept her going. She seemed to age suddenly. Once steady, she was moved to a rehabilitation center, where months of therapy gradually restored some function, but she would never fully become who she was before.

Watching my sister Carol take on the role of caregiver gave me a new appreciation for her. After years of depending on our mother, she now cared for her completely — cooking meals, managing medications, driving her to appointments, encouraging her to bathe, and cleaning up after accidents. It was exhausting work, and I knew I didn't have the strength to do it myself.

Each of us had a different role in our family. I couldn't control how things happened, and maybe it was never my job to keep everyone together.

Part Five
When Love is Not Enough

~1~

The haunting sound of cicadas echoed in my dreams. I moved through my days on autopilot.

"What do you do all day?" my mother-in-law asked.

It sounded more like an accusation than a question and made me feel inadequate.

A few days later, I enrolled at the local community college and signed up for a night class.

The first evening I stepped into that classroom, I felt out of place. I could still hear my high school counselors in my head.

"You're not college material."

I sat in the back with a notebook and a pen, my heart thumping.

To my surprise, I loved the course. When I got my first A, I stared at the paper as if it belonged to someone else. Maybe I *was* college material.

Tests were different. Even when I knew the answers, my mind went blank. Somehow I learned to work through it — breathe, slow down, keep going anyway.

I took one class at a time while my children were at school. I was in no rush. For the first time in years, something belonged to me.

When people asked what I was doing now, I smiled and said, "I'm a student."

~2~

I was beginning to feel more confident, but my daughter was still struggling to find her place. I kept searching for Annmarie's unique talent — something to boost her confidence. I signed her up for Brownies, softball, and even karate. She resisted all my attempts to help her grow. Nothing seemed to work.

I wanted her to be popular at school and have many friends like my cousin Katie — even if I had to create the opportunities myself. Convinced that all she needed was a friend, I became more involved in the school. It seemed to work. We started meeting other families.

One day, Annmarie said she made a new friend.

"Her name is Crystal. She let me join her for lunch today."

"That's fantastic. Why don't you ask Crystal if she'd like to come for a sleepover this weekend?"

Full of hope, I saw the sparkle in Annmarie's eyes. Maybe this was the answer to her insecurities. I installed a phone in her room so she could talk to her new friend.

One day, I saw Annmarie on the phone, tears streaming down her face. "Crystal made friends with the new girl at school. She doesn't want to be my friend anymore." Girls can be ruthless.

To reduce the discomfort caused by social pressure, I sometimes pulled her out of school.

"I'm here to pick up Annmarie Corrigan," I told the school receptionist. "She has a dental appointment."

With a skeptical look, she grabbed the intercom microphone. "I need Annmarie Corrigan for early dismissal."

When Annmarie entered the office, her face showed panic.

"I don't want to go to the dentist."

"We're not going to the dentist," I whispered. "We're going shopping."

Annmarie giggled with delight.

Those moments felt like victories. Annmarie looked up to me as her hero, and I did everything I could to please her.

But then one day, Edward and I heard Annmarie crying in her room.

We stood outside the door and listened as she talked aloud, saying she wanted to die.

Horrified, we pulled her out of public school and enrolled her in a private school. It was expensive, but we found a way to pay for it.

At first, the private school seemed to be the perfect solution. It had a small class of around five students, and the teacher provided one-on-one instruction. There was no pressure like in public school.

Annmarie seemed less depressed and performed better in her studies.

The financial strain kept growing, and after a year, we had to move her back to public school.

I told myself things would get better. But the problems we were facing were only beginning.

At least, that was what I always told myself. I needed to believe Annmarie loved me. The alternative was more than I could bear.

-3-

The change began when she turned sixteen. The warmth disappeared from her eyes. She moved through the house with tense shoulders, her responses sharp. If I reached out to her, she pulled away. A wall formed between us, stone by stone.

I told myself it was normal. Adolescence. Hormones. I even read an article linking stress hormones to memory and emotional regulation. At the time, it felt like the perfect explanation.

She accused me of being disappointed in her. She used that idea like a shield, deflecting every attempt to help. I was blamed for her insecurities. No matter what I did, I couldn't prevent her from slipping into self-destruction.

We were different in that way. While she fought me with everything she had, I spent my adolescence eager to please. Her resentment and vulnerability were tearing me apart. Countless times, I opened my heart, only to have it crushed into the dirt.

My mind said one thing, but my heart said another. Still, I couldn't give up. I'd take her on shopping sprees at the mall or to lunch, where she had my full attention.

In my heart, I knew it wouldn't make her love me more, but it usually improved her mood, even if just for a little while. For a few hours, she would even smile. However, by dinnertime, her mood would turn sour again, and her depression would return.

Eventually, we stopped going to the mall together. I went alone instead, scanning the racks the way I always had — tops, pants, dresses — my arms filling with things I imagined might make her happy.

One afternoon, I waited in line at Macy's with clothes draped over my arm and watched a mother and daughter ahead of me. The girl leaned into her mother as they talked, smiling up at her with an easy devotion that felt like a language I didn't speak. It was the kind of relationship I had longed for with my own mother — the one I had hoped to have with my daughter.

Something in my chest tightened. Maybe if I were a better mother, I could give my daughter the nourishing love she desperately needed, a love I struggled to express. Instead, I found myself emotionally distancing from Annmarie.

Before it was my turn at the register, I stepped out of line, hung the clothes back on a rack, and left the store.

Although it felt like a declaration of my independence, it also made me sad. I cried during the drive home. I drifted back to the times when we were close.

-4-

I promised Annmarie Paris when she turned sixteen, and I kept my word. We spent a week there before taking the train to London.

Annmarie quickly noticed the children.

At the metro stations, families huddled in corners to keep warm. On the streets, children ran toward us with their hands out, begging for money. We couldn't go five feet without being stopped.

Despite my warnings, Annmarie emptied her purse.

"You can't keep giving them money," I said softly. "Their parents take it and send them right back out."

"I can't ignore them," she said with tears in her eyes.

"Why don't we go to the store and buy a bag of lollipops?" I suggested. "When the children run up to us, we'll hand them out."

That seemed to work well, and soon, she started carrying bread to give to the old men who slept in the stations.

One afternoon, a disheveled man limped toward us, mumbling in French. Without hesitation, Annmarie offered him her loaf.

He stared at it—then exploded. He shouted, waved his cane, and spat curses we didn't understand.

We stood there stunned, then rushed away.

I told her she didn't need to give away every piece of herself.

She nodded, but I wasn't sure she believed me.

We took dozens of pictures that week—smiling on bridges, laughing at cafés. Proof of a time when we were close.

I believed we would always find our way back to each other.

It was the last trip we made before everything changed.

When we came home, discontent hung in the air like lightning waiting to strike. We moved around each other in the same house like strangers. Any wrong word could set her off. If I tried to comfort her, she pushed me away. If I became firm, she called me cruel. Every attempt missed the mark.

I started noticing small things.

Annmarie began wearing long sleeves even on hot days.

When I asked if she was feeling hot, she shrugged and said she liked them.

One afternoon, I saw blood on the cuff of her sweatshirt.

Soon after, I found a bloody towel in her room.

I stood there holding it, trying to understand what I was seeing.

I didn't want to believe it. But the towel in my hands was proof.

My first instinct was to call my mother. I wanted to confide in her, but as I grew up, I couldn't even say I had a headache without her accusing me of a mental disorder.

Although I had hinted at my daughter's problems before, I couldn't tell my mother the full extent. I couldn't tell her Annmarie was a cutter. Somehow, she would blame me, confirming my fears that I was failing as a mother.

The school got involved when some of the other girls told the teacher what she was doing. They suggested seeing a therapist.

At first, it seemed to help, but I never knew what she divulged behind the closed door.

I wanted to be there for my daughter during the session, but she wanted to speak to Annmarie alone, hoping she might be more open.

It hurt that she didn't trust me, but I accepted the advice.

Waiting alone outside the office, I wrung my hands. When the session ended, Annmarie walked past me without making eye contact. The therapist offered a polite smile but said nothing.

-5-

Not long after, I began noticing more changes. Annmarie began dressing in what she called Goth fashion. She lined her eyes in heavy black, making her pale face look almost hollow. Doc Marten boots seemed better suited to Frankenstein's wife than to my tiny daughter. I might have accepted it as a phase or a statement of independence, but something deeper had changed. She began ditching school and lying.

Someone had taken my sweet, innocent child and left behind an angry young girl.

Soon, the signs were harder to ignore.

Her eyes sometimes looked glassy, and a familiar sweet, skunky smell clung to her clothes. My instincts suggested she might have been smoking pot. When I asked, she said, "Daddy smokes pot all the time."

I had no answer for that.

Every morning, there was a loud argument to get her to school.

"I hate you!" she yelled and watched my face as if waiting to see what I'd do.

Her words cut me as if she had used her razor to make my emotions bleed. With my heart in pieces, I swallowed hard and walked away without reacting.

At night, I'd fall into bed with her words still echoing in my ears. But after a few hours, my eyes would snap open, and anxious thoughts would take over. I'd listen for sounds from her room. If it was silent, I'd check to see if her door was locked—a sure sign she was inside. When I could open it and saw her bed empty, my heart would race with worry. I wondered where she was and if she'd come home safe.

People advised me to be stricter, so I set boundaries, but each time I did, she pushed back harder. Even small comments set off her anger. I was afraid of conflict, so I backed down.

Meanwhile, the cutting continued.

Annmarie kept drawing razors and other sharp objects across her arms, even after counseling. She tried to hide the cuts with a bracelet made from ceiling fan pull chains. I suspected she was hiding other injuries beneath her clothes.

The school counselor recommended I attend a weekly meeting called "Tough Love."

Tough Love made me feel better for a while. I posted the Parents' Bill of Rights on the refrigerator, but I found it in the sink one day, the blackened edges left for me to see.

That night, we sat down to dinner like any other evening. She picked up a steak knife and slowly ran her finger along the edge.

A line of red dots appeared and merged into a crimson line. She looked into my eyes with defiance and raised the knife to cut another finger. I quickly jumped up and grabbed it from her hand.

"Why are you doing that? Why do you want to hurt yourself?"

I barely slept that night. I lay awake wondering what she might do next.

-6-

The next morning, after she left for school, I went into her room. I noticed new holes in the walls, made by her fists or Doc Martens. I searched for sharp objects—opened drawers, looked under the mattress, and inside shoes—anywhere she might hide something dangerous. I found sharpened keys, razors snapped from their plastic handles, a pocketknife, and even the metal strips from her music CD covers.

I gathered them into a bag and took them out of the room.

Before I left, I noticed the necklace I had given her. During an argument, she ripped it off and threw it to the floor. A second later, she dropped to her knees, crying, pawing at it as if she'd destroyed something she couldn't bear to lose.

Later that day, she found out I had taken her cutting objects. She yelled that she wished she were dead and ran to her room. The lock clicked before I could get to the door.

Something slammed into the wall. A drawer was yanked open. There was a crash. Then everything went silent.

"What are you doing?" I asked.

No answer! Panic rose, and I banged on the door.

Edward heard the commotion and ran upstairs. "If you don't open this door," he yelled, "I'm taking it off the hinges."

Still, there was no response.

He ran to the garage for a screwdriver.

By the time the hinges loosened, sirens were blaring up the street.

When the door finally came off, the police were already there.

Annmarie had called 911.

Putting us on trial.

I told the officer, "Our daughter was trying to hurt herself."

"I'm sorry, ma'am. She's seventeen. Legally, she's an adult. She has rights!"

"She can do whatever she wants, even under my roof?"

"I'm afraid so, but that doesn't mean you're not responsible for her if she does something unlawful," the police officer warned.

After the police left, the house felt different.

-7-

Love and resentment coexisted within her. She needed me, but at the same time, she resented needing me.

Out of desperation, I started writing her letters. It felt safer because I could carefully think about what I wanted to say. After leaving one in her room, I waited for her to respond, but when she found it, she tore into me. "You can't help me," she screamed, "so stop trying! I hate you! And I hate this house!" I snapped.

"Get out if you don't like it here!" I yelled and shoved her clothes into the same garbage bag I had given her to clean her room.

Annmarie looked at me for a moment. I had lost control, and I couldn't take it back. Barefoot and barely dressed, she grabbed the bag and ran out the door. I followed her, apologizing for my outburst and begging her to come back, but she didn't even look back.

After she left, the house felt empty. I kept replaying the moment in my mind — my voice, the bag, the slam of the door.

That night I didn't sleep. I sat up listening for the door. I kept picturing her out there — bare feet, no coat, nowhere to go.

Love alone — no matter how fierce — cannot protect a child from every storm.

I had lost her!

Part Six

Diagnosis

The tragic death of Princess Diana in a car crash dominated the news and shook the world. Until then, the British royal family had barely registered in my life, aside from the spectacle of Diana's wedding to Prince Charles. But after the headlines faded, the stories deepened. Commentators dissected her loneliness, her struggles, her desperate need to belong. Reports spoke of erratic moods, eating disorders, and self-harm—pain hidden for years behind a practiced smile.

As I listened, I couldn't help thinking about Annmarie. The stories about Princess Diana felt uncomfortably close.

At five, she struggled to show frustration. Shyness followed her everywhere—ballet classes, gymnastics lessons, and class performances. While other children leapt forward, she stayed in the corners, unsure, shrinking away from attention.

Something was wrong with my daughter. I just didn't know what it was. I stayed up late searching the internet for answers. One diagnosis kept appearing. Borderline Personality Disorder.[2]

Bookstore shelves offered answers—or at least the illusion of them.

---

[2] Diagnostic and Statistical Manual of Mental Disorders
   DMS5 Fifth Edition

One title stood out: *Lost in the Mirror* by Dr. Richard A. Moskovitz.[3] He wrote about fragile identities.

Self-esteem has always been unstable in my family. It began with my mother and trickled down through my sisters and me—women who doubted themselves, stayed too long in unhappy places, and never quite believed they deserved more.

From the moment she was born, I was determined that Annmarie would be different. Determined to build her up, I encouraged her every time I saw a spark of interest in something or a hint of talent. I believed confidence could be learned—that if she found something she loved and was good at, everything else would fall into place.

It didn't.

Moskovitz's book discussed children who learned to withdraw inward.

Doubts began to creep in. Maybe I was at fault. Had I sheltered her too much? Had I made it easier for her to hide from the world instead of facing it?

Each theory felt like another question aimed directly at me.

Dr. Moskovitz also stated that identity forms early and is shaped by experience. He suggested that early trauma might leave invisible scars.

My mind flashed back to the incident at the

---

[3] Lost in the Mirror: An Inside look at Borderline by Richard A. Moskovitz M.D.

dentist's office when she was just a toddler. To the straps. To her frightened eyes. To her screams as they took her back to perform root canals on her baby teeth — procedures no child should ever have to experience.

Had something broken then?

I closed my computer and took out the photo albums. Page after page. Year after year. Until I reached her thirteenth birthday.

Balloons stuffed into nightgowns. Girls laughing and posing like Dolly Parton.

Annmarie in the center of it all — bright, silly, alive.

I stared until my eyes blurred.

Where did she go?

-2-

Two weeks later, the phone rang. It was Annmarie.

"I just wanted to let you know I'm still alive."

A wave of relief washed over me.

"Are you okay? Where are you?"

"I'm at a friend's house."

Friend? She once told me that I was her only friend.

"Please come home."

"I can't. I'll call you tomorrow," Annmarie promised without leaving a clue as to where she was staying.

When the line went dead, I sat there holding the phone long after the dial tone returned.

The next day, she called again.

"Annmarie, I've been really worried about you. Please tell me where you are, and I'll come pick you up."

"No. I'm not ready."

"Sorry, I don't want to pressure you. I'm just worried."

"Don't worry. My friend's parents are nice. They take in kids who have no home."

"But you have a home!"

"I'm staying!"

Sensing her anger, I stopped pushing.

"Alright," I said quietly.

She called every night.

Initially, she spoke about her new friends. Gradually, she lowered her defenses.

After she left the house, a man saw her crying and offered to find her a place to stay.

"I trusted him, Mom!"

"What happened?"

"At first, he was nice. He even took me to Pensacola to get a tattoo."

"You left the state?"

"I'm stupid—I know!"

She was quiet for a moment.

"He raped me."

"Oh, my God. Did you call the police?"

"No! I can't!"

"Why not?"

"You don't understand. He's the head of a gang. I shouldn't have told you. Forget what I said."

I didn't push. I couldn't risk losing her again.

After three weeks of frustrating conversations, she finally agreed to come home. I noticed more scars on her arms from cutting.

"Why do you cut yourself?" I asked flatly, trying to keep the emotion out of my voice.

"I feel empty inside. It's like I'm numb."

Her response puzzled me. "Doesn't it hurt?"

"No. Cutting *stops* the pain."

"Are you trying to kill yourself?"

"No. It's the opposite. It's a release. It makes me feel alive."

I didn't know what to say, only that I couldn't handle this alone. So, I suggested counseling.

-3-

Annmarie drew hard on her cigarette, then stubbed it out against the concrete wall outside the counseling center.

She had admitted to smoking, and I pretended not to care.

All my hope was in that building. They were professionals. They could help her deal with the rape.

She signed in at the front desk. When the receptionist called her name, Annmarie headed down the hallway, leaving me in the waiting area.

Minutes stretched into something that felt endless, although it was only half an hour.

A woman stepped out and whispered something to the receptionist. They both looked at me.

I stood and walked toward the desk just as the receptionist hung up the phone.

"Is something wrong?" I asked. "Is my daughter all right?" I moved toward the hallway.

The receptionist rose quickly. "Please have a seat. Someone will be out to speak with you," she said firmly.

Before I could answer, a sheriff's deputy came up to me.

"I'm sorry," the receptionist said. "We believe your daughter is a suicide risk. She's being hospitalized under the Baker Act."

"The what?"

Then Annmarie appeared — hand

She was handcuffed.

The deputy led her past me and into the patrol car. They were the authorities — I couldn't oppose them.

For a moment, she looked at me through the open door. I thought she might say something. Instead, she raised her hand and flipped me off.

She thought I set her up. That this was a trap.

The car drove away.

Why didn't I do anything? Why didn't I speak up? I could have demanded that they couldn't take her — that she was my baby, my child, mine.

I stood there, frozen, paralyzed by guilt.

If only she had talked to me, listened to me, maybe she wouldn't have run away, wouldn't have been raped, or wouldn't have been dragged away.

Finally, I went back inside.

"Where are they taking her?" I asked. "And what is the Baker Act?"

"Your daughter is being taken to the Riverside Outpatient Center for mental health evaluation," the receptionist said. "There's a seventy-two-hour hold before you can see her." She wrote an address on a pad and handed it to me.

They were the medical professionals. They knew what was best for her.

In shock, I left the building. All I had done was try to get her help. I never imagined it would end like this.

-4-

Annmarie was lying on the bed in the psychiatric ward when I entered. Drool ran down her chin. She didn't move, but her eyes followed me, wide and frantic.

"Oh, my God! What happened to you?"

She sobbed and tried to speak. Her tongue seemed too heavy for her mouth. The words came out stiff and slow. Her voice sounded like it was coming from somewhere far away.

"They're drugging me. Please... get me out of here."

"I'll find out what's going on."

At the nurse's station, I asked for the doctor, but the nurse told me he had left for the day. She took my number and promised to have him call me.

I went back into Annmarie's room and sat beside the bed.

"I'm sorry, honey. The doctor isn't here. I'll talk to

him tomorrow. Can you hold on until then?"

She nodded, crying softly. "Okay."

The doctor agreed to stop the drugs, but he wouldn't release her, stating she wasn't stable.

Once the drugs wore off, she could use the phone.

"Mom," she whispered. "Can you bring me cigarettes?"

"All right," I said, even though I had sworn I would never support her habit.

I found her in the recreation room and handed her three packs of Marlboro cigarettes.

Other patients leaned against the walls, laughing, smoking, and passing the time.

Later that day, I was allowed to sit in on one of her therapy sessions. It didn't take long for her edge to come back, and I became the target of her attack.

"My mother never hugs me," Annmarie said flatly.

"That's not true!" I said, reaching for her.

"Don't touch me!"

I pulled back.

We used to be inseparable. When she was young, I'd carry her on my hip. She followed me everywhere. Somewhere along the way, that closeness faded.

Now, there was a gap between us—one that widened each day.

"I don't get along with my mother," she went on.

"Why do you think that?" the counselor asked.

"I'm not the daughter she wants."

"What kind of daughter is that?"

"Smart, outgoing, normal." She shrugged. "I'm a disappointment."

"That's not true," I said. "All I want is for you to be happy."

"She never lets me speak for myself."

"I want you to speak for yourself," I said. "You just shut down."

"You just want to control me."

I froze. I had always tried to give her a voice. When she started kindergarten, I even let her choose her school outfits. At first, I thought it would build confidence, but it only seemed to confuse her. Eventually, I had to step in and make the decisions.

The counselor watched us quietly.

"She's twisting everything," I said. "I'm trying to help her make better choices. After she stormed out of the house, she never came back. She was raped."

Annmarie turned toward me.

"My mother thinks it was the first time I was raped, but it wasn't. I was raped in my own room."

"What?" I stared at her.

She looked down.

"I don't remember that," I whispered. "Where was I?"

"You were at school or shopping."

"Why didn't you tell me?"

She shrugged.

"Who raped you?"

"Remember when I went to the mall with my friend Jenny?"

"Yes."

"We met some guys. One couldn't go home, so I asked if he could sleep on the couch. I told you he was

Jenny's cousin."

"Yes, I remember."

"He entered my room while we were listening to music. He kissed me, then began to undo my clothes. I told him to stop. I tried to push him away, but he was too strong."

"Why didn't you scream?"

"I was afraid I'd get in trouble."

"For what?"

"For lying that he was Jenny's cousin. For letting him stay."

I closed my eyes. "You wouldn't have been in trouble."

She didn't answer for several moments.

"You always think I'm messing up."

"That's not true."

"You're disappointed in me. I know you are."

"Maybe you're disappointed in yourself," I snapped.

The counselor shifted in her chair, and the room went quiet. "Are you disappointed?"

I stared at the floor.

Am I disappointed in her? What parent wouldn't be if their child was hurting themselves and refusing to go to school? I had to hold that back. I couldn't say it out loud.

When the session ended, my head throbbed.

I walked out feeling empty, as if something inside me had been split open and revealed.

Seventy-two hours later, the hospital discharged Annmarie.

Nothing had really changed.

She came home with pamphlets and referrals and a new appointment for outpatient therapy. But the anger was still there.

Sometimes, it felt like we were making progress. She talked, or laughed, and stopped slamming doors.

Then something small would set her off, and everything would unravel.

Living with Annmarie was like riding a storm. Some days, she was fragile and lost. All I wanted to do was protect her. Other days, she was sharp and cruel, and I felt myself harden in response. Guilt always followed. I'd lower my boundaries and make excuses to smooth things over. Anything to keep the peace.

In the hospital, she'd made a new friend. A girl with a drug problem. They exchanged numbers and promised to meet.

I wasn't comfortable with the friendship, but said nothing. Cutting was still her coping mechanism. Therapy was my last hope. Maybe someone else could reach her.

While we searched for answers, the rest of her life was unraveling.

-5-

Annmarie wasn't thriving in a traditional high school. She was almost two years behind on her credits. Eventually, she stopped trying. Mornings were battles I couldn't win. Some days, she didn't even get out of bed.

I couldn't let her quit, so I found an alternative school for students with behavioral challenges. It was forty minutes away, and I had to drive her there.

She lasted less than a month before quitting. The only option was a GED.

Around that time, she became interested in getting a driver's license. It seemed like progress, so after she passed her test, I agreed to help her buy a used car — if she found a job and paid for the loan and insurance.

She got a job at Arby's, and we bought an older Honda Accord for $2,000. As motivation, I promised to match her savings to upgrade to a newer model.

In her uniform, she looked almost ordinary. The tattoos and scars were hidden. She looked like any other teenager, except for the knee-high Doc Martens.

For a while, she worked, studied, and earned money, but she didn't save any of it. Instead, she spent her cash on new tattoos and piercings. First, she got a belly button ring. Then, to my horror, she got her tongue pierced. The last piercing was through her eyebrow.

Late for work every day, she finally lost her job.

The car payments became our responsibility. We revoked her driving privileges, except for school.

Annmarie unraveled, and the cutting returned.

We agreed to loosen the restrictions if she found another job.

When she started a cashier job at the mall, I felt encouraged — then a new crisis hit. She tested positive for tuberculosis, maybe from handling cash at the gift store. No one knew for sure.

She had been quarantined for months and wasn't allowed to leave the house. A health worker came daily to give her medicine.

She spent her days smoking in the yard. Cigarette butts covered the lawn.

At first, I complained about the mess. Then I stopped. If I said the wrong thing, it might drive her to the razor.

So I bent down and picked them up one by one.

Annmarie was cleared by her doctors and got back into her grunge routine. She earned a GED, but holding a job was more difficult.

While I tried to keep her life from falling apart, I was also trying to hold my own together.

It took me twelve years to earn my bachelor's degree. Sometimes, it was exhausting trying to balance my studies with Annmarie's problems. Other times, it was a relief and a break from the daily stresses of motherhood.

But Annmarie wasn't there to celebrate. She refused to come, unaware of how close I had come to quitting or how many times I had thought about giving up. Maybe she believed it had been easy for me.

My mother sat next to me at graduation. It was one of those rare moments when my mother and I stood together, sharing my achievement. I was thankful she was there to witness it.

The photos of me in my cap and gown looked almost unreal. I sent a copy of my degree to my father. Proof, at last, that I was college material after all.

He called to congratulate me. Then he asked, "So,

what are you going to do with it?"

The question hit me hard. I didn't have an answer. Success always made me uneasy. It meant stepping into the spotlight and proving I was good enough. Maybe I was scared of losing approval.

Before I thought about getting a job, Edward asked me to help him grow our exhibit business. He needed someone to handle the administrative side.

With my insecurities at their peak, it felt safer, so I said yes and hung the diploma on the wall in my new office. It was easier to frame my achievement than to test it. On the wall, it couldn't challenge me.

Looking back, I started to realize how much my struggles were connected to my family patterns, though at the time, I didn't understand any of it.

Part Seven

The Roots of Codependency

Shortly after her twenty-third birthday, Annmarie packed her bags and moved out. I had always imagined that day would come with a wedding, not quietly, with boxes carried to a small apartment. Even though it hurt to watch her go, I knew she needed space to start her own life.

Letting go was more difficult than I expected. I couldn't separate what I felt from what she needed. In the end, I helped in the only way I knew how — paying the deposit, buying dishes, pots, and silverware — small things meant to make an empty place feel like home.

Once she moved out, the tension between us eased. Distance softened what closeness had strained. She called every day just to talk, and I treasured those conversations more than I admitted. She kept working in the family business and seemed, at least on the surface, to be finding her footing.

That was when she met Charles.

He was warm and confident, full of Southern charm. I couldn't quite picture them together at first, but I told myself that mothers don't always understand what their daughters see. He was older, already a father, steady in ways that reassured her. Before long, he moved in, and soon they were engaged.

Marriage, I hoped, might give us a new way to relate to each other — less as mother and child, more as two women sharing similar lives.

Planning the wedding brought us closer again. Annmarie wanted a beach ceremony, and I instantly thought of a hotel we loved in Florida, a place filled with memories from happier vacations. Helping her plan felt like being welcomed back into her world.

I missed traveling with her. Once she got married, those spontaneous mother-daughter trips would probably fade away, so we decided to take one last trip together before the wedding. For her birthday, we chose Aruba.

On the first night, I was exhausted, but Annmarie wanted to listen to music at the hotel bar. She promised she'd stay only an hour. I went upstairs, uneasy but trying to respect her independence.

When I heard her key in the door later, relief washed over me — until she told me she had met a young man traveling with his mother who wanted to show her the nightlife in town.

Every instinct in me tensed. I wanted to say no right away, but she reminded me she was an adult.

"Then, I want to meet them," I said, quickly getting dressed.

In the bar, the young man sat next to an older woman who introduced herself as his mother. They were polite, but something felt slightly off — a tension I couldn't quite identify. We talked briefly before Annmarie excused herself to the restroom.

Minutes passed. Then more.

Something wasn't right.

The woman suddenly stood up and offered to check on her, but I stayed close behind. From outside the stall, I could hear Annmarie vomiting. The door was locked, and I couldn't reach her. Panic filled my chest as I called her name and asked someone to get help.

By the time security opened the door, she was unconscious.

They brought a wheelchair and helped us back to the room while others assumed she had simply had too much to drink. But Annmarie insisted she had only had a Dr. Pepper. As we pieced things together, fear replaced confusion. The couple had vanished without a trace.

-2-

In the days after we returned home, we talked about Aruba less and less. I dismissed it as a strange vacation experience, something odd but already behind us.

Annmarie seemed happy and excited about the future. Maybe the trip was just a reminder that she was growing up and stepping into a life I could no longer control. So I pushed aside the unease and focused on the wedding. Planning gave us something hopeful to hold onto, a way to move forward together.

Debra threw herself into the preparations, buying twenty pounds of candy-coated almonds for favors and gowns for herself and her daughters.

I placed a three-thousand-dollar deposit on a reception hall in Florida, and plans quickly came together. Annmarie hired a dressmaker to make a gown from sketches she had drawn.

Before the next payment was due, my phone rang. Annmarie was crying so hard I could barely understand her.

"Mom, I'm in trouble," she said. "Charles tried to hit me. I'm scared."

"Stay where you are," I told her. "I'll send Daddy to get you."

Two hours later, she came through the door and announced that the wedding was called off. For a moment, I thought about the money already spent, but the thought quickly faded. All that mattered was that she was safe.

After the wedding was called off, the house drifted into a tense quiet. The dress sketches were stored away, the reception hall deposit forgotten, and the candy almonds sat untouched on the kitchen counter. We avoided talking about Charles, as if silence alone could erase what almost happened.

Annmarie moved through the days slowly, sleeping late and helping at the business when she could, trying to figure out what came next. I told myself this was only a pause — that she would regroup, find her footing again, and life would return to something recognizable.

But beneath that hope lingered a familiar worry, the sense that we were standing on the brink of another change we couldn't yet see.

It arrived sooner than I expected.

Usually, when Annmarie came home, she would bring a stray cat. This time, she brought something heavier — she was pregnant.

She told me she was thinking about having an abortion. My feelings were mixed — worry for her future, fear of what was coming, and the understanding that the decision was hers alone.

The drive to Planned Parenthood was quiet. Outside, protesters shouted and held signs, their voices loud on a day that already felt fragile. Inside, four other girls sat in the waiting room, three with their moms and one with her boyfriend. The room smelled of disinfectant and desperation.

One by one, the girls were called into the counseling office. When it was Annmarie's turn, I decided to stay behind. There were magazines on a table, and I stood up to pick one up to distract myself. Flipping through the pages of the Christmas edition of Ladies' Home Journal, I saw models in holiday sweaters smiling accusingly from the pages. I threw it aside and tried to relax, letting the music fill my ears and pull me out of the moment. Finally, the door opened.

When she came out, she was holding a sonogram.

Instead of counseling her about abortion, they showed her a film. She saw babies at different stages of development, tiny fingers and toes moving in their protected environment. By the time she walked out, her decision had changed.

Motherhood. All its promises of perfection and doing things right stood before her. How could she resist?

Panic flickered beneath my calm. She had no job or home of her own, and I knew much of the responsibility would fall on us. Still, I respected her choice. Maybe motherhood would steady her. Maybe this would be a new beginning.

Edward and I had grown accustomed to quiet routines and were starting a new chapter in our marriage, but we made room again. I set simple rules — small efforts to keep order as we adapted to living together.

As her belly grew, her ideas about the type of mother she wanted to be also expanded.

"When my baby is born," she said. "I'll raise it differently than you did."

Her words initially hurt, but I recognized something familiar. I once shared a similar sentiment about my own mother. Every generation believes it can improve by fixing what came before.

I began to realize how much of my parenting was motivated by my desire to give her what I never had growing up.

For a while, we settled into a gentle routine. Doctor's appointments filled the schedule, tiny clothes began to appear folded in drawers, and conversations turned to baby names and nursery colors. I let myself believe we were headed toward calmer waters. Pregnancy seemed to give Annmarie something to hold on to.

As the weeks passed, the excitement faded. She became more anxious. I can see the familiar shadow of depression creeping back.

Mornings stretched later into the day, and small tasks started to feel overwhelming. I told myself it was exhaustion, hormones, the normal weight of impending motherhood. Still, a familiar unease returned — the sense that something beneath the surface was slipping beyond my control.

Annmarie slept later each day and rarely left her room.

By the time her due date was just weeks away, I could no longer ignore it.

"You can't just hide in your room all day," I complained. "Get out of bed."

"I'm sorry if I'm a burden to you."

"I never said that. I can't understand why you won't help yourself."

"Maybe I should give Charles another chance. At least my baby would have a mother and a father."

"If you think going back to Charles will be different, you're fooling yourself. You're just looking for a short-term solution."

"Why are you so negative?" she asked, touching a sore spot. I'd heard that often from her father, and it never escaped her ears. Like a hammer, she kept using the term to rile me.

"I'm sorry you feel that way." I took a long breath and dug deeper for the lessons I'd learned in my codependency group.

"I can't change how you feel about me, but please keep it to yourself. Labels are hurtful."

"You don't understand! He's threatening me."

"Why do you keep talking to him?"

"If I don't, he may fight for joint custody. He says he wants to raise our baby half the time, and I'd better get ready to pump my breast milk."

"He's not going to take your baby away."

"I can't take that chance."

"Right now, you and the baby have to come first."

"I don't know," Annmarie whined. "I'm confused."

"You're not cutting anymore, are you?"

"No!" she said while avoiding my gaze.

I suspected she was trying not to cut, but based on everything I had read, it didn't seem likely. When stress overwhelmed her, a look came into her eyes that warned me she might slip back to the razor. I had to ignore the fresh scars because there was nothing I could do to stop her. The fact that she showed them on her arms, when she could have easily hidden them on her stomach or legs, told me she was crying out for help.

"Your father and I can only offer advice, but you are an adult. You don't have to take it."

It finally started to sink in. I couldn't make Annmarie make good decisions. The only thing I could do was be there to lift her if she fell. Constantly worried about her emotional needs, I had prioritized her life over my own. After years of trying to solve her problems, I had to step back.

After that conversation, something between us changed. I stopped trying to solve every problem or anticipate every crisis. Instead, I focused on small, practical things — doctor's appointments, folded laundry, meals left warming on the stove. The arguments grew less frequent, replaced by long stretches of uneasy silence.

As the weeks passed, the urgency of conflict gave way to waiting. The baby's arrival began to overshadow everything else. We moved carefully around one another, both of us conserving energy for what was coming, as if the house itself were holding its breath.

-4-

During the last few weeks of Annmarie's pregnancy, we waited. Looking forward to becoming a grandmother, I felt less anxious than I had when I was pregnant with my children. Whatever they did with their lives would be okay with Grandma. I remembered how my mother interacted with my babies. She would give them bubblegum, earning her the nickname "Bubblegum Grandma." It was so different from how I saw her growing up. My children loved her most, and my mother seemed to value loyalty. She carried it too far, though. Just as she did with her children, she told each of her grandchildren they were her favorite. It caused problems when they were old enough to compare, and my children felt betrayed, especially my son. He thought that all the women in our family were mentally disturbed.

As I reflected on my mother and the ways love passed — sometimes imperfectly — from one generation to the next. We stood at the start of another chapter. Soon, I would no longer just be a mother but a grandmother, witnessing the same hopes and mistakes unfold from a different perspective.

Baby clothes filled the drawers, the hospital bag sat ready by the door, and every phone call made my heart race. Without noticing when exactly, anticipation overtook reflection, and our focus shifted entirely to the moment we knew was coming.

-5-

October was hot as the Indian summer wound down in Georgia. Edward was on a business trip, so it was just Annmarie and me.

Every night we cooked dinner together and took long walks around the block because we had heard it would induce labor.

Halfway through our walk, Annmarie doubled over and put her hand on her stomach.

"Are you all right?"

"No. I've been having these pains all day. It's getting worse, though."

"You might be in labor!"

"It's too soon. My due date is next week."

"Babies don't have a schedule," I laughed. "Let's swing by the house and grab the suitcase you packed for the hospital."

For the next three hours, I stayed beside her as she walked the hospital halls, breathing through waves of pain that came closer and closer together.

The nurse examined Annmarie and declared it was time. When they wheeled Annmarie into the delivery room, the nurse stopped me from entering.

"Only one visitor is allowed in the delivery room," she said. "The father is already here."

"But I'm supposed to be my daughter's coach."

"I'm sorry. You can stay in the delivery waiting room. It's very comfortable. There's a television, and you can use the internet. I'll keep you informed on your daughter's progress."

Resentment consumed me as I thought of Charles playing the daddy role. Where was he while I endured her hormonal episodes for nine months? I had done all the hard work. Now he waltzed in to take the credit.

My mind drifted back twenty years to when I experienced the same birthing process as my daughter. I never expected the chaos that one baby girl could cause. Disappointed, I sank into the plush leather seat and sipped a complimentary coffee.

It was time for me to let go. I could no longer make decisions about my daughter's life.

Two hours later, the nurse came back, smiling widely. "It's a girl."

Holding my granddaughter for the first time, I felt both wonder and unease. A new life had entered our family, full of possibility, yet I couldn't ignore how familiar everything seemed — the hopes, the fears, the quiet promises mothers make to do things differently.

Watching Annmarie hold her daughter, I understood something I had spent years resisting. Every generation believes it will do things differently. And every generation tries.

End Note

For most of my life, I dismissed the word *codependency*. I thought it was a term for other families, not mine. I thought it meant weakness or clinginess. Only later did I understand it as something far deeper—confusing love with responsibility.

Much of what shaped me began with my mother. She gave endlessly, but love often arrived tied to guilt and obligation. Approval depended on how well I anticipated her needs. I learned to read moods, smooth conflicts, and avoid my father's anger whenever possible.

Looking back, I can see how early that pattern began. As a child, I stepped into the role of caretaker without realizing it. I wanted to soothe, to fix, to make things better. Without intending to, I carried that same urgency into my relationship with my daughter. I believed it was my job to rescue her.

I never could.

One unexpected result of my daughter's struggles was the realization that many women in my family were caught in the same patterns. We were connected in a complicated knot, and I often wondered where it all began. Maybe with my mother and the wounds she never spoke about. Maybe those wounds quietly passed to her daughters, each of us finding different ways to manage needs that were never fully met.

For years, whenever my daughter cried, I rushed toward her room, certain it was my duty to make everything right. Only later did I understand that I was answering an older call — the frightened child inside me who had learned to stay awake, listening for trouble, believing it was her job to keep the peace.

"Tough love" slowly took on a new meaning. It was no longer about correcting my daughter's choices or controlling her life. It was about protecting my own well-being. Letting go felt unnatural; responsibility had defined me for so long that releasing it felt like failure.

Understanding codependency didn't end my struggles, but it changed my direction. I learned that love and self-respect can exist together. Caring for myself felt unfamiliar at first, almost disloyal, yet it became the only way forward.

This time, instead of trying to fix everything around me, I finally learned to sit beside that child — and let us both rest.

Letting go was not a failure.

It was freedom.

Thank you for reading Queen of Hearts

Please help the author by posting a review on Amazon.
Feedback is very much appreciated by emailing your
questions and comments to lamaisonpublishing@gmail.com

Suggested Reading

Borderline, bipolar, or both? Frame your diagnosis based on the patient's history. *Current Psychiatry*
http://bit.ly/2RB1DoR

Shame: The Core of Addiction and Codependency
Psych Central - Darlene Lancer, JD, MFT
https://psychcentral.com/lib/shame-the-core-of-addiction-and-codependency

Coping with Narcissists. Numb, Disconnected & Dissociated
www.youtube.com/watch?v=oC2x79P-TUo

What is Dissociation - Webmed
https://www.webmd.com/mental-health/dissociation-overview#1

Low Self-Esteem and Codependency
Psych Central - Darlene Lancer, JD, MFT
https://www.dummies.com/health/mental-health/codependency/low-selfesteem-and-codependency

The Family Dynamics of Patients with Borderline - David M. Allen, M.D.
http://bit.ly/38kf4jv

DYSTHYMIA (CHRONIC DEPRESSION) AND CODEPENDENCY
https://psychcentral.com/lib/chronic-depression-and-codependency/

NMDA - neurotransmission as a critical mediator of Borderline Personality Disorder by Bernadette Grosjean and Guochuan E. Tsai, Canadian Medical Association
https://www.ncbi.nlm.nih.gov/pubmed/17353939

Asphyxia
www.aboutkidshealth.ca/En/ResourceCentres/PregnancyBabies/NewbornBabies/CaringfortheVeryIllNewbornBaby/Pages/Brain-and-Behaviour-Problems.aspx

Childhood Trauma Permanently Scars the Brain and Boosts the Likelihood of Depression
The Intellectualist - Julie Glaser
http://bit.ly/2G6Docx

Strap him down or knock him out.
Is Conscious Sedation with Restraint an Alternative to General Anesthesia? British Dental Journal 14 February 2004
https://www.nature.com/articles/4810932

Psychosocial Stages
Erik Erikson
www.simplypsychology.org/Erik-Erikson.html

Traumatized Children:
How Childhood Trauma Influences Brain
Development Bruce D. Perry, M.D., Ph.D.
www.childtrauma.org
Traumatic Stress Effects on the Brain
J. Douglas Bremner, M.D.* US National Library of
Medicine
www.ncbi.nlm.nih.gov/pmc/articles/PMC3181836

Manifestations of Borderline Personality Disorder
Part two: High-functioning in Borderline Personality
Disorder
www.beyondtheborderlinepersonality.wordpress.co
m/category/high-functioning

Enmeshment: Symptoms and Causes
BY FULSHEAR TREATMENT TO TRANSITION
https://www.fulsheartransition.com/enmeshment-
symptoms-and-causes

Lost in the Mirror: An Inside Look at Borderline
Richard A. Moskovitz, M.D.

Diana in Search of Herself
Portrait of a Troubled Princess - by Sally Bedell
http://www.nytimes.com/books/first/s/smith-
diana.html

Diagnostic and Statistical Manual of Mental Disorders DMS5 Fifth Edition

Why Borderline Personality is more common in Women
http://www.borderlinepersonalitytreatment.com/bo rderline-personality-disorder-women.html

How Do Maladaptive Behaviors Worsen Social Anxiety Disorder? Very Well Mind Arlin Cuncic http://bit.ly/2hKYjXd

Adrenaline, Cortisol, Norepinephrine:
The Three Major Stress Hormones, Explained Huffington Post http://bit.ly/2NFkk9A

Hormones and Borderline Personality Features
Milagros Evardone, Gerianne M. Alexander, and Leslie C. Morey Department of Psychology, Texas A&M University, College Station, TX www.ncbi.nlm.nih.gov/pmc/articles/PMC2700629

Stress Hormone Hinders Memory Recall
Cognitive Neuroscience Society https://www.cogneurosociety.org/cortisol_memory

Effects of Cortisol on Memory in Women with BPD
Role of comorbid post-traumatic stress disorder and major depression. Wingenfeld K1, Driessen M, Terfehr K, Schlosser N, Fernando SC, Otte C, Beblo

T, Spitzer C, Löwe B, Wolf OT.
www.ncbi.nlm.nih.gov/pubmed/23171911

BORDERLINE WAIFS AND UNSUNG HEROES
Rescuing the Woman Who Doesn't Want to Be Saved.
Shari Schreiber, M.A. www.GettinBetter.com

We Can't Save Our Mothers from Their Pain -
Bethany Webster 2014 – 2016
http://bit.ly/30AiQ5B

Enmeshment: Symptoms and Causes
BY FULSHEAR TREATMENT TO TRANSITION
http://bit.ly/2R5Q4a2

The World of the Borderline Mother
And Her Children by Christine Lawson, Ph.D.
www.borderlinepersonalitydisorder.com/resources/
media-library/cal

**Emotional Manipulator: Why we become
codependent in our Childhood**
How & Why We Develop Codependency.
www.youtube.com/watch?v=qkIP4ThAlME

**The Continuum of Self – Self Love Deficit Disorder:
Where do you fall on the Continuum of Self**
Ross Rosenberg M.Ed., LCPC, CADC, CSAT
http://bit.ly/37aj45V

Welcome to Co-Dependents Anonymous

www.CoDA.org

Borderline Personality Disorder
John M. Grohol, Psy.D.
www.psychcentral.com/lib/borderline-personality-disorder

The Family Dynamics of Patients with Borderline -
David M. Allen, M.D.
http://bit.ly/38kf4jv

Borderline Personality Disorder Symptoms
Steve Bressert, Ph.D.
www.psychcentral.com/disorders/borderline-personality-disorder-symptoms

**Other books by
Florence St. John**

Entangled
Searching for the Shire